UNMASKING THE RADICAL'S BLUEPRINTS TO SILENCE CHRISTIANS, PATRIOTS, AND CONSERVATIVES

PERRY STONE

AMERICA'S APOCALYPTIC RESET

DISCOVER STUNNING PROPHETIC PATTERNS OF HISTORY THAT PREDICT AMERICA'S FUTURE

AMERICA'S APOCALYPTIC RESET

AMERICAS APOCALYPTIC RESET

Published by Voice of Evangelism Ministries
P. O. Box 3595
Cleveland TN 37320
423.478.3456
www.perrystone.org

Printed in the United States of America

ISBN: 978-0-9855372-9-6

Cover Design & Layout: Michael Dutton

CONTENTS

INTRODUCTION

FREE EAGLES AND CAGES DON'T GET ALONG

Three of America's founders (Thomas Jefferson, John Adams, and Benjamin Franklin) suggested that the American Bald Eagle should be the centerpiece of the Great Seal of the United States. Their reason being eagles are "Strong and independent; they are survivors. They are majestic, bold, and faithful. They are a symbol of strength and determination."[1]

Many years ago, a young boy was visiting a large zoo with members of his family on a guided tour. The group arrived at the bird section, where the lad noticed three beautiful, majestic eagles secured inside an inescapable massive metal-net fence. They were confined in one spot. Inside the cage were beautiful trees, lush vegetation refreshed with a delightful waterfall, creating a natural environment for them to live in and enjoy. They were being watched, well-fed, and cared for. Two eagles were perched on a large tree branch, seemingly content with their life in captivity. The third bird, however, was using his strong, large claws (talons), tightly gripping the large metal-mesh cage that imprisoned him, continually flapping his wings, shaking that side of the enclosure. It was as though he hoped to create an opening to free himself from his metal prison.

Observing the expressions on the faces of the people, the zoo guide said, "I think it is clear that you can tell the difference between the eagles that were born in *captivity* and the eagle that was born *free*."

The boy never forgot this statement. The nature of any eagle is to be free, to fly with the wind high above the pollution. Those born in confinement have no concept of this freedom. Therefore, free-born eagles and cages do not get along.

For centuries, American citizens have loved their freedoms. Millions of families have immigrated to this "land of the free and home of the brave." They came by ships and planes, some risking their lives to escape the cages of dictators, religious persecutors, evil and corrupt governments, escaping from Communism and Fascism. Many Muslims and Middle East Christians seek asylum from radical and dangerous Islamic regimes. For most oppressed people, America would be their first choice, as America represents freedom. Today, many descendants of those immigrants who evaded those oppressive nations are becoming worried. They see similar anti-freedom parallels occurring in our national and state governments that their parents and grandparents fled from decades ago.

I have an older friend who lives in California but was born in Romania prior to it becoming a Communist nation. He has, with a great burden, recently noted the radical, political, and social changes in America. He said that the ways in which conservative politicians and business owners are being persecuted (their information and products publicly banned, some fired from their jobs, and their personal accounts frozen) are the exact same tactics used by the Romanian Communists prior to their complete control in 1947, especially before the rise of the twenty-four-year Romanian Dictator, Nicolae Ceausescu (1965-1989).

America is only one of 195 nations that are presently recognized in the table of nations. However, America is the world's leading Gentile empire-nation and has been since the end of World War II, when America introduced the nuclear age to the rest of the world.

Today, America is at a four-lane crossroads. These four lanes include political, religious, moral, and cultural transitions. Legislators, including Presidents supported by the Supreme Court, have passed federal laws that permit the very things that God rejects. They legalized specific sins, once permitted and committed by ancient cities that led to their destruction by fire. Included in this list is the city of Jerusalem in AD 70. Jerusalem's judgment was predicted by Christ 40 years prior to the event. Christ exposed their sins, chiefly, shedding the blood of the righteous.

In Matthew 23:34, Christ spoke of "prophets, wise men, and scribes" that His own people had "killed, crucified, persecuted, and scoured." Jesus reminded His audience that their ancestors slew the High Priest, Zacharias, between the porch and the altar (Matt. 23:35). Mistreating righteous believers continued after Christ's ascension with the martyrdom of the first early church leader, Stephen. He was stoned to death for preaching a sermon to prove that Christ was the promised Messiah (Acts 7). Acts 12 records the death of the Apostle James by the decree of King Herod. King Herod also plotted to behead the Apostle Peter after Passover had ended. The book of Acts records Paul's missionary journeys, documenting his physical beatings, including being stoned in Lystra along with numerous arrests just for preaching the message that Christ was the true Messiah. It was God Himself who said to Jerusalem and Judea, "Enough is enough." Between AD 66 to AD 70, the Almighty removed the protective hedge over Jerusalem and the Temple, allowing the enemies of Israel, namely the Roman Tenth Legion, to break through Jerusalem's defensive gates. Battering rams weakened the city's stone walls, breaching places once thought impossible.

The Jewish historian, Flavius Josephus, observed a series of strange signs years prior to Jerusalem's desolation. In his book, War of the Jews, he was an eyewitness to the entire war. He wrote:

> *"Moreover, at that feast which we call Pentecost, as the priests were going by night into the inner court of the temple as their custom was to perform their sacred ministrations, they said that, in the first place, they felt a quaking and heard a great noise, and after that they heard a sound as of a great multitude, saying, "Let us remove hence."*
>
> – Josephus Antiquities, War of the Jews, Book 6, Chapter 5, Paragraph 3

Other strange signs began occurring, often during festivals. Josephus tells his readers of a cosmic sign, a great comet seen over Jerusalem for one year. Modern scientists have identified that comet as Halley's comet, which, throughout history, is often seen a few years before wars break out. Josephus wrote that during the night, a great light shone from heaven upon the altar. The most frightening sign was at the sixth hour of the night, the gate of the inner temple (made of brass and was very heavy, requiring twenty men to open and shut) was seen opening of its own accord. The unskilled interpreted these signs as good omens, indicating that God was supernaturally shutting the doors on their Roman enemies, preventing them from entering the temple compound. In their perception, the temple was being supernaturally protected. However, Jerusalem's wise men warned that God Himself supernaturally opened the huge temple gate, departing from His temple, now leaving the sacred compound unprotected. This meant that Israel's enemies would soon invade, unhindered, bringing a catastrophic conclusion to the holy city. The sins of Israel, including shedding innocent blood, had sealed the doom of the world's most recognized, spiritual city.

THE AMERICAN PROPHECIES

Today, many Americans are spitting in God's face. They accept all forms of sin as normal, now believing that truth is only what you believe it is, removing all moral absolutes. The older, more patriotic, and religious Americans are passing away, including hundreds of thousands of our faithful, God-fearing, flag-waving patriotic seniors and veterans who have succumbed to the COVID virus.

Many of America's founders believed that America's birth was a sovereign plan of God, marked with prophetic destiny. Clearly, our history runs parallel with similar patterns and cycles of ancient Israel and Imperial Rome. Israel, as a nation, arrived at its burning end in the year AD 70 and was non-existent until rising from the ashes of the Holocaust in 1948. As for Rome, the mighty empire eventually collapsed from within. Historians suggest taxation, uncontrolled immigration, plagues, political division, and political corruption sealed the doom of the Western Empire. If Rome's Senators, those ruling years before Rome's fall, could rise from their graves, spending one hour in the U.S. House, Senate, and the Oval Office, they would scream warnings to all elected legislators to learn from Roman history as America is repeating the same mistakes and political nonsense that eventually collapsed the Republic. If religious Jews living a few years prior to Jerusalem's destruction could rise from the dust, spending one hour with leaders of both political parties, their message would be summed up in three words, "Turn or burn."

America's prophecies also follow similar chastisements and judgments parallel to the days of Noah and Lot. In Noah's day, a catastrophic disaster destroyed the earth. Among the pre-flood global population, "the earth was filled with violence," and "all flesh had corrupted itself." Only one older man, Noah, remained on earth and was "perfect in his generation" (Gen. 6:11-13). God was grieved that He had created mankind. The flood concluded mankind's creation (from Adam to Noah). God introduced a *Global Rest* using Noah's three sons, whose children and their descendants formed 70 nations after the destruction of the Tower of Babel (Gen. 11 and 12). Another Global Reset is coming. This reset is not a "God thing," but a satanic strategy to reorganize and reprogram the world's population by creating a godless planet. This includes an economic reset that will eventually be controlled by the Antichrist.

To make the New World Order work, without opposition, creating a global reset, the United States must either submit to all of the globalist agendas or be radically changed from within by forcing the population to follow their new set of rules.

In this detailed teaching, I have researched some amazing prophetic truths. My hope is that as you read, the eyes of your understanding will open to comprehend prophetic times. This moment in history reminds me of a statement that an angel made to Daniel in Daniel 12:4, indicating that in the time of the end, "Many will run to and fro, and knowledge will be increased." This knowledge is spiritual knowledge to understand the final prophecies. This teaching emphasizes the Prophecies of America, including patterns found among ancient cities and empires from scripture that are beginning to repeat again as an indication that the return of Christ will occur in the future. The truth and information in this book are for Christians, American Patriots, conservative-minded American's who have asked themselves, "What is going on, and what can we do about it?" The information you will hear will answer both questions.

Two ancient empires had an eagle as their emblem, Imperial Rome, and, in the Old Testament, the Babylonian Empire (Ezek. 17). This book will especially compare Babel and Babylonian parallels to events occurring now.

Referring back to my opening paragraph, the American Bald Eagle is the emblem on the Great Seal of America. Printed on the back of every dollar, on the left talon of the eagle, are olive branches that represent peace. Printed on the right talon are arrows that represent war. Our freedoms, represented by the eagle, are at risk. The cages of radical democratic-Socialism, a new Marxism, and the patterns of Fascism are being prepared in America. It is not a time for olive branches but a time to pick up the arrows and fight back.

May the eagle that is born free, break through its cage of bondage and fly high again.

CHAPTER 1

ANCIENT BABEL-GLOBALISM NOW TAKING EFFECT

The first biblical record of a global-type government is recorded in Genesis chapter 11. After the universal flood in Noah's day, Noah's sons and descendants began to repopulate, as fear of a future watery destruction faded in their minds. Mankind slowly migrated off the mountains, eventually setting up towns and building cities in valleys near rivers that provided water for agriculture. In Genesis 10:8, a strong leader named Nimrod attracted a large following in the plains of Shinar, located in this day and age, in what we know as Iraq. One of the earliest and most popular cities was called Babel, where Nimrod and the people constructed a massive tower called "The Tower of Babel." The historical events surrounding the city of Babel and its famous tower have parallels to the global ideology being propagated by today's international globalists.

In scripture, Nimrod is called "a mighty hunter before the Lord" (Gen. 10:9). Some Jewish interpreters teach that this phrase actually reads, he was "in opposition to the Lord." His name, Nimrod, is believed to mean "rebel."[1] The Jewish historian, Josephus, indicates that

Nimrod turned the people from God, teaching them that their happiness depended upon their own courage. He also changed the government into a tyranny, as he could not turn the people from God unless he brought them into a constant dependence on his power. Josephus wrote that the people who followed Nimrod "esteemed it a piece of cowardice to submit to God."[2]

Moses documented Babel's formation and history in Genesis 11:1-4:

> *"And the whole earth was of one language, and of one speech. And it came to pass, as they journeyed from the east, that they found a plain in the land of Shinar; and they dwelt there. And they said one to another, Go to, let us make brick, and burn them thoroughly. And they had brick for stone, and slime had they for mortar. And they said, Go to, let us build us a city and a tower, whose top may reach unto heaven; and let us make us a name, lest we be scattered abroad."*

The city called Babel was designed to be the headquarters of a new economic and political order. The concept was based upon the idea that if all the people would unite economically, politically, and spiritually, there would be nothing they could not accomplish (Gen. 11:6).

Our world is continually changing. The true and only God is being omitted from society and politics as man becomes his own god. For many, authentic Christianity is viewed as a religion for weak cowards. Nationalism, such as "Put America First," has been thrown in the swamp by wealthy elitists who want to expand their own personal influence and wealth, gaining greater control over the "ignorant" masses. According to the ancient biblical prophecies, nations will merge into coalitions, eventually requiring a global economic system. Toward the time of the end, this system will be controlled by one main central bank, promoting one currency (more like a globally approved cryptocurrency). In his apocalyptic vision, John saw a coalition of nations called "the kings of the east" (Rev. 16:12), which included a two-hundred-million-man army (Rev. 9:16). Another future coalition is the Antichrist and his ten-nation confederacy, which was seen in Daniel's vision (Dan. 7:7-24) and confirmed hundreds of years later in John's vision of the Great Tribulation (Rev. 13:1; 17:3).

Every nation connected with global trade prints and sets the value on their individual currencies. The United States operates using dollars, the British use the Pound, the Japanese print Yen, Israel uses the Shekel, and so forth. There are 180 world currencies, and most of these can be exchanged for dollars, using a rate of exchange. Each day, investors trade huge sums of foreign currency, determining the exchange rates. These are the rates you get in exchanges and banks when you are changing money from one currency to another.[3] Under a New World Global Order, one main currency or method of monetary exchange will emerge, placing all nations on the same monetary level.

Before Noah's flood, men began building cities, each with their separate forms of government and leadership. The first city mentioned in scripture was when Adam's son (Cain) married, he built a city naming it after his son Enoch (Gen. 4:17). Cain settled "east of Eden" past the easternmost river boundary of the Euphrates River (Gen. 2:14; 4:16). Today, this would be the nations of Iraq and Iran. All cities worldwide were destroyed during the deluge and needed to be rebuilt after the floodwaters receded.

THE FIRST GLOBAL CAPITAL

The area of Babel, later known as Babylon or the Babylonian Empire, was the first recorded organized form of government. After Noah's flood, men were fearful of living in the lower valleys for fear of drowning by a second flood. However, Nimrod convinced multitudes to follow him into the plains of Shinar. The Jewish historian, Flavius Josephus, wrote:

"These first of all descended from the mountains into the plains, and fixed their habitation there; and persuaded others who were greatly afraid of the lower grounds on account of the flood, and we're sloth to come down from the higher places to venture to follow their examples."

– Josephus Antiquities of the Jews,
Book 1, Chapter 4, Paragraph 1

Instead of living in separate colonies, as was the pre-flood pattern, a large population chose to unite in one location. There is historical proof of Nimrod rebelling against God. Nimrod was a strong rebel that attempted to turn men against God as alluded to by Josephus: He wrote:

"He also said 'he would be revenged on God, if He should have a mind to drown the world again; for that he would build a tower too high for water to be able to reach, and that he would avenge himself on God for destroying their forefathers.'"

– Josephus Antiquities of the Jews,
Book 1, Chapter 4, Paragraph 2

FOUR BABEL PATTERNS REPEATING TODAY

There are the four patterns seen in the story of Babel that will reemerge in men's attempt to create a global system designed to control and monitor all of humanity. First, during the tower of Babel era, the population spoke *one language*, which helped unite them in this new form of government. There are 1,600 languages spoken across the globe. However, because of the British Empire and colonization, the English language is a universally spoken language. Babel allowed one man, Nimrod, to lead the people in their economic, agricultural, and construction programs. In reality, Nimrod was the first type of king-dictator the world had in almost 18 centuries. Most historians believe the people were also united around one form of religion, which was not the worship of the true God, but was a female deity and her son called Thammuz, an idol later alluded to by the prophets in Israel (Ezek. 8:14). Finally, the most important aspect of the Babel effect was that if the people remained united, there was no restraint to what they could do. Their confidence was in their own power and ability, with no need for the true God. This is a type of modern humanism, which is defined as "an outlook or system of thought attaching prime importance on human rather than divine or supernatural matters."[4] Men can build towers without God, but cannot stop God from bringing down what they build.

WE NOW HAVE GIANTS

An interesting and somewhat mysterious part of the pre-flood and post-flood generations is the fact there were giants scattered throughout the earth that were instigating violence, creating evil imaginations, and had corrupted all of mankind. Recalling the pre-flood days, Moses wrote:

> *"There were giants on the earth in those days, and also afterward, when the sons of God came in to the daughters of men and they bore children to them. Those were the mighty men who were of old, men of renown. Then the Lord saw that the wickedness of man was great in the earth, and that every intent of the thoughts of his heart was only evil continually."*
>
> – Genesis 6:4-5 (NKJV)

Christ predicted that "as it was in the days of Noah, so shall also the coming of the Son of Man be" (Matt. 24:37). Giants were on earth before and after the flood, until finally, this race of dangerous demi-gods was annihilated by David and his four mighty men (2 Sam. 21:16-22).

Some scholars believe that the giants were the "seed of the serpent" (the offspring of fallen angels and the daughters of men), a phrase God Himself alluded to in Genesis 3:15. Josephus, in his Antiquities of the Jews, noted that the giants were intimidating in size, and their voices frightened the Israelites.

> *"There were till then left the race of giants, whose bodies were so large, and countenances so entirely different from other men, that they were surprising to the sight, and terrible to the hearing..."*
>
> – Josephus, Antiquities of the Jews,
> Book 5, Chapter 2, Paragraph 3

The story of David and Goliath reveals that no Israelite in the entire army wanted to challenge this ten-foot-tall Philistine champion. Even King Saul was too timid to take on this threatening giant from Gath (1 Samuel 16-17).

Since history is repetitive, with past events repeating in future cycles and parallel patterns, if there were "giants" in Noah's day, there will be some type of *giants* in our time, as the same signs from Noah's day will replay themselves prior to Christ's return (Matt. 24:38).

It is interesting to note that the major social media tech companies, who are in total control of what a person can and cannot say on their media platforms, are called "Tech Giants." These companies are mainly located in the ultra-liberal Silicon Valley in Northern California. These include Apple, Google, Facebook, Amazon, and Microsoft. These are five of the largest (giant) corporations that control the information highway. Farhad Manjoo, a tech columnist with the New York Times, in an internet interview heard on Fresh Air, called these tech companies the "frightful five," writing that they were more powerful than many governments in the sense that in modern American life, it is nearly impossible to live without them. They all work on artificial intelligence.[5] These are the world's modern giants.

In the Old Testament, in the time of King Saul, and later, King David, there were five giants remaining in Israel: Goliath (1 Sam. 17), Saph, Lami, Ishbibanob, and the giant from Gath (2 Sam. 21:16-22). Israel had five giants, and America has five "tech" giants. Before Noah's flood, the giants were called "mighty men" (Gen. 6:4), which in Hebrew is Gibborim. In Moses' day, there were *five* different groups of giants surrounding the Promised Land. They were the Rephaites (also known as Zamzummites), Anakites, Horites, Caphtorites, and Avvites (Deut. 2:19-23 NIV).

The five main giants listed in the Old Testament controlled the main *gates* or entrances into Israel. The north entrance was Bashan, and the south entrance was Gaza, the giants in the *west controlled the coastal areas of Israel,* and the east was the land located in Jordan. In Israel, the Philistines controlled five western coastal cities: Ashkelon, Ashdod, Gath, Gaza, and Ekron. These five cities became spiritual strongholds and non-stop battle zones between the Philistines and the Hebrew people living in Israel.

In a strange twist, three *western* states, California, Washington, and Oregon have *five extremely liberal cities* not far from the Pacific coast with liberal mayors, governors, and House and Senate representatives elected by the population. These five cities are Portland, Seattle, San Francisco, Los Angeles, and Oakland. The prophetic parallel is that Israel struggled with the giants and five Philistine cities, always intimidating, threatening, or harassing the Hebrew people. The five giants established a "mental control" of dominance, just as conservatives and Christians in America teaching "controversial" truth are seeing negative responses, including silencing and a bit of intimidation from the five tech giants.

In another point of interest (although not at all prophetic), the giants were positioned at the main entrance points to the Promised Land. These were also the main roads serving as trade routes for caravans. Controlling the trade routes would enable them to disrupt the *income* in and out of Israel. These routes were considered the main "gates" to and from the land. One man who is responsible for the founding of Microsoft computer systems and software is named Bill Gates. Microsoft is the world's biggest software company and one of the world's most valuable companies in the world. Gates' net worth has been estimated to be $129 billion dollars, placing him in the top tier of the world's wealthiest men.[6]

In January 2021, shortly after an intrusion into the United States Capitol, these Tech Giants took it upon themselves to ban individuals, organizations, and national media leaders who were in any way supportive of Trump. Other forms of social media forums that were pulling followers from these left-leaning giants, namely Parlor, were banned from their hosting platforms to help silence voices opposing their liberal-political and social agendas.

BUILDING TOWERS

The central feature in the city of Babel was the massive *tower* constructed by Nimrod and his followers. In Genesis, Moses gives Torah readers the tower's history:

> *"And they said, Go to, let us build us a city and a tower, whose top may reach unto heaven; and let us make us a name..."*
>
> – Genesis 11:4

There are several thoughts as to the purpose of this tower. Josephus wrote that Nimrod and the people were fearful that God might choose to send another deluge, bringing a second global destruction. Nimrod and his followers built a tall ziggurat, a building with a square base and winding steps ascending to the top. Josephus said this was to escape another flood and provide safety at the top. Apparently, these post-flood citizens paid no attention to the promise God gave Noah, pledging to never again destroy the earth by water. As a visible representation of God's promise, He gave men the rainbow as a sign of His covenant agreement (Gen. 9:13-15). Some believe that the top of the tower, built to reach heaven, may have also been connected with some type of astrological worship, which was popular in the land of Ur in the time of Abraham.

The tower was the centerpiece of the city. They successfully accomplished the building process, building it faster since the people spoke "one language," which implies that their building completion was due to their ability to communicate in one language. The *tower and communication* were linked together.

The prophetic parallel of the tower of Babel and the towers of today are the tens of thousands of *phone towers* that we see in cities, towns, and on mountains throughout the fifty states, connecting phone *communications* across the nation. As men construct these towers, reaching upward into the sky, these concrete and metal, man-made communication towers are necessary to connect signals from wireless phones. Also, a metal *computer case* is known as a computer chassis *tower.* These towers contain the components of the computer. I am also reminded that on 9-11, the two World Trade Center Towers were attacked, bringing the massive skyscrapers to the ground. These towers housed offices and businesses connected with world trade and corporate cooperation.

WHAT HAPPENED TO BABEL?

The story of Nimrod, Babel, and the tower took a strange turn. We read in Genesis 11:5-7 NKJV:

"But the Lord came down to see the city and the tower which the sons of men had built. And the Lord said, 'Indeed the people are one and they all have one language, and this is what they begin to do; now nothing that they propose to do will be withheld from them. Come, let Us go down and there confuse their language, that they may not understand one another's speech.'"

The plans of the Nimrod administration, to remove God from the minds of the people and to form a new world order, becoming the king of the world, suddenly came to an unexpected halt when God Himself judged the hearts and plans of the post-flood population. The tower, which represented one language and one government, collapsed by a divine act of God Himself. Complete *confusion* suddenly swept throughout the city as the people were no longer united politically, economically, or socially.

The confusion was a result of God removing their one language, dividing their ability for unified communication (Gen. 11:7). The Hebrew word here for *confounded* (KJV) is *balal*, meaning *to mix, confound, and mingle.* This is why scholars note that "babel" in Hebrew refers to *confusion,* making reference to the confusion of the languages that *occurred.*[7] The end result caused the people to be "scattered abroad on the face of the earth" (Gen 11:9).

THE BRICKS AND THE STONES

The most overlooked pattern, and seldom, if ever taught link of Babel with our time, is the reference concerning the "brick" and the "stone" used in the building of the tower. The reference is in Genesis 11:3. The KJV reads as follows:

> *"And they said one to another, go to, let us make brick, and burn them thoroughly. And they had brick for stone, and slime had they for mortar."*

In today's society, this "brick and stone" strategy designed by our current progressive "Nimrods," as they sit in their position of power in state and national governments, is to control the general "blue-collar" American population. In Babel's building process, instead of using stone, the builders molded and baked their own bricks. Stones are taken out of the earth. Each stone is uniquely created, consisting of various sizes and colors. Stones consist of white limestone, black basalt, red rose, and many brown colors. Adam was created from the earth, and the colors of the earth's stones are similar to the different skin tones of men scattered throughout the earth. God create the stones just as He created all colors of men and women.

In Babel, under the global order of Nimrod, the builders made bricks instead of providing natural stones. Bricks are all made from the same molds. Each has the same length, width, height, color, and look. They are baked in ovens to harden them. The "brick system" represents the systems of Socialism, Communism, and Fascism. The idea is to place the common people on the same level by having them dress similarly, eat the same basic foods, and robotically follow a pre-determined set of rules. When Hitler seized control of Germany, he demeaned and degraded the Jewish people, murdering over six million innocent souls in a form of ethnic cleansing. His goal was to create a special Aaryan race of blond-hair-blue-eyed Germans, a super race superior in strength and intellect to all others. Hitler blamed Germany's pre-1933 economic woes on Jewish bankers and the Jews in general. Years of German economic suffering only fueled the flames for a future Jewish Holocaust.

In the United States, there is a select network of political Nimrods, egotistical know-it-all legislators, attempting to get rid of the individual and free-thinking *stones* of liberty that formed the bedrock of

America, uprooting hundreds of years of history to lay a new foundation with their own bricks. To these atheistic, anti-Christian, Bible-rejecting groups, the Holy Bible is an antiquated relic whose inspired text needs to be either changed or banned, but certainly not taught publicly or accepted by the majority. In their twisted Babylonian mentality, Christians are an extreme fringe within western society and need to be disciplined into silence, allowing no voice on the public airways. They have dusted the cobwebs off the *playbook* of the Soviet Marxists and democratic-Socialists of 1933-Germany to resurrect the ghosts of history's past.

THE BONHOEFFER SPIRIT

When the five media giants began a conspiracy to silence conservative voices, I was reminded of one bold minister in Germany, Deidrick Bonhoeffer. He was a noted radio minister. In 1933, two days after Hitler was installed as Chancellor, Bonhoeffer began warning the German people of falling into the idolatrous cult of Fuhrer (Hitler) worship, the dictator who would eventually seduce and mislead the German nation. Bonhoeffer could see the handwriting on the wall and knew the more power Hitler and the Reich received, the less freedom the professing Christians would have. While speaking on his national radio program, he was suddenly cut off in the middle of his urgent warning.[8]

In 1934, the Confessing Church was organized. By that time, most Germans were being seduced into believing that Hitler was a savior that would restore economic stability and raise up a new German Empire, named The Third Reich. Some deceived German-Christians were considering Hitler as the head of the Christian Church. Since the name, Third Reich, held certain negative opinions with some, the Nazi's banned its use in the press and changed the name to National Socialist Germany or the Greater German Reich. This Babel spirit arose from its ancient tomb, as evident when the Nazis annexed Austria, they began speaking of "one people" and "one leader." They believed their new German kingdom would endure for a thousand years.

Just as God warned about Babel, many Germans believed that if they were united in this new kingdom with a new Aryan race, there was nothing restrained from them — nothing they could not *accomplish*.

When dictators attempt to reform a nation to their own standards, they will always plot to silence any opposing voices. This is accomplished by banning them over all forms of media, arresting them, and, in some instances (as in North Korea and China), placing them in camps where the opposition often dies of sickness, hunger, or torture. Bonhoeffer was arrested and died just a short time before the Allies liberated Germany from the menace of the Nazi regime.

Bonhoeffer spent years in and out of different countries, working secretly with the German Resistance. By 1941, he was forbidden to speak or write in public. By 1945, he was sent to a concentration camp. On April 9, 1945, he was executed by hanging. He was 39 years of age. His last words were, "This is the end — for me, the beginning of life." [9]

Just as Nimrod did, Hitler tapped into the Babel spirit, constructing a temporary man-made empire using bricks of Fascism. Years later, it was blown to pieces.

THE SLIME CONNECTION

In the Genesis-Babel report, the bricks were held together by "slime" (Gen. 11:3). In this context, the word *slime* literally refers to a dark tar-like substance (found in that region) used to hold bricks together (similar to cement) and is also an effective water-proofing agent. Oil is abundant in this region, and geographically speaking, there was plenty of "slime" available. It was "slime" that held all the bricks in place.

Using slime for an analogy, when I was a child in the early 1960s, America was a different nation. Prayer and Bible reading were permitted each morning in public school. In those days, adults born in America loved this nation and its traditions. We flew and pledged allegiance to the flag, stood for the National Anthem, sang Christmas songs in public school assemblies, and the majority of our citizens had some church affiliation. Politics were divided between "yellow dog" Democrats and Republicans, but the calls for violent confrontations to score political points were virtually non-existent.

Today, too many elected officials hold to ideologies mixed with slime! This slime includes lust for power, greed for money, and unwillingness to challenge voter corruption. It has been exposed and proven that corrupt politicians will look at a camera, lie under oath, cheat, and accept under-the-table illegal bribes and still not be held accountable. *It is hard for the fox in the hen house to be held accountable by other foxes!* Another weasel will not prevent a fellow weasel from stealing a chicken if his fellow thief is willing to share the meal. The old-timers from the mountains had a phrase for a person they distrusted, who manipulated people for their own gain. They were called "slime balls."

The globalist-socialists sitting in the U.S. Capitol, who have aligned with globalists in China, Russia, and Europe, are willingly undermining the solid rock foundation upon which American beliefs and moral instruction was built. This includes tearing out by the roots, our Judea-Christian tree that has brought forth the fruit of blessing for centuries.

THE BRICKS OF EGYPT

The Hebrew nation was exiled in Egypt for several hundred years. These Israelites were a righteous, covenant-people, dwelling among a civilization who worshiped false gods and burnt incense in idol temples. The Hebrew people were oppressed by cruel taskmasters and egotistical pharaohs. The Egyptian government was in control of the food supplies and the job market, including forcing the Hebrews to work unpaid overtime. Healthcare was non-existent, and healing was practiced by "so-called physicians," using garlic, lizard blood, and other strange "cures" that produced no results. The Israelites, who were once a free people, were taken into bondage by a new pharaoh who had no intimate relationship or spiritual understanding of the religious nature of the hundreds of thousands of Hebrew people. To Pharaoh, the Hebrew God was just another god and nothing special.

Among the Hebrews were 600,000 men over age twenty, capable of forming a sudden uprising (Exod.12:37). This possibility instilled fear in the Egyptian palace. The government eventually initiated population control, as Pharaoh instructed a nation-wide *after-birth* killing of all male Hebrew infants. This is the same evil act that some states are presently legalizing. By killing the male infants, there would be fewer Hebrew infant births in the future. This was an early form of population control (Exod. 1:16-22). The government selected taskmasters to control the workforce. The Hebrew word for *taskmasters* could be interpreted as "tax collectors" in today's modern English. To the Egyptians, the Hebrew people were a cheap form of labor for their building projects. Moses noted that the Hebrew slaves were building treasure cities for the Egyptians. The Israelites lived moderate lives, while the Egyptian elite lived in huge mansions of marble and stone.

To many globalists and most progressives, abortions are necessary to save the planet and reduce the human population. The opening line on the National Library of Medicine, under the heading, "Role of Abortion in control of global population," reads, "No nation desirous of reducing its growth rate to 1% or less can expect to do so without the widespread use of abortion." It continues, "...Abortion is essential to any national population growth control effort." The article notes that in America, there are 426 abortions per 1,000 live births.[10] Today, our pharaohs work in the abortion industry, supported by the laws passed by the Supreme Court in 1973. They can "double-dip" when being paid for the abortion by selling the aborted infants' organs for research.

The Israelites in Egypt were instructed to make *bricks out of clay*. Each person had one job, was paid one fee, and provided a specific amount of food and a house to live in. Today, we would say the entire population was dependent upon *government assistance*. In Egypt, there were six types of available foods: fish, onions, leeks, garlic, melons, and cucumbers (Num. 11:5). After forty years in exile, when Moses, a new and unknown leader arrived and demanded that the king of Egypt release the Hebrews from his iron grip, he was rejected. It required ten plagues, the tenth concluding with the death of Pharaoh's son—heir to the throne—to humble the entire Egyptian nation into submission to God's will.

BRICKS REPRESENT SOCIALISM AND COMMUNISM

Socialists believe personal and corporate wealth should be distributed equally. Said another way, the "haves" must support the "have nots." The biblical commandment from Matthew 25 is for believers, or Christians, to clothe, feed, and help the poor, visit the sick, and those in prison. However, the scriptures rebuke busybodies and disorderly individuals and teach that if a man can work but refuses, he should not eat (2 Thess. 3:10). In America, some who can work prefer not to, choosing to live off government assistance. When building our large O.C.I. facility, the contractor hired a young man at $10.00 an hour to keep the site clean. He quit the job after two weeks after calculating that he could stay home, receive government financial assistant, clearing up to $16.00 an hour.

Socialism eventually fails when the government runs out of other people's money. The radical-left hopes to control a nation of bricks. They want to control a nation of living, breathing robots. These robots must be "yes people," never questioning any new laws, never exposing corruption, and never pointing out the countless double standards. They must be similar to sheep going to the slaughter, never opening their mouths.

A FUTURE NEW WORLD ORDER

What has been called the "New World Order" is perfect imagery of Nimrod's Babel and a city called Babylon from the time of the biblical prophet Daniel. When the European Union was formed with strong economic nations joining the coalition (eventually introducing a new currency called the EURO), prophetic scholars pointed to the possibility that this modern coalition included nations from the former Imperial Roman Empire. This new unification, new currency, along with other interesting developments set the prophetic world on edge, as well-respected prophetic scholars began announcing that this union was the ten kings alluded to in Daniel and Revelation, inferring that they would form the eighth and final prophetic kingdom (Rev. 17:11).

A man named Peter Bruegel painted three unique works of art on the subject of the Tower of Babel. The circular base of the tower was in the form of a Roman Coliseum. The European Union used the tower of Babel as their emblem with the theme, "Many people and one voice." It is interesting that the E.U. Parliament building in Strasbourg, France, is shaped in the form of the Tower of Babel, similar to this painting.

The interesting link between the E.U. and the tower of Babel theme is found in Revelation chapters 17 and 18, dealing exclusively with Mystery Babylon, a "city ruling over the kings of the earth" (Rev. 17:18). The Babel theme appears in Genesis 11, in the book of Daniel, concluding with a spiritual-economic Babylon at the time of the end in Rev. 17 and 18.

CHILDREN OF BABYLON

Early Marxists and Communists understood that to gain the hearts of a generation, seeds must be planted during childhood and early youth. The family of my Jewish-Israeli tour guide, Gideon Shor, originally lived in the Soviet Union. Gideon told me that prior to the 1917 Russian Revolution, Russia was a strong Christian nation. Communism needed to defeat the ideas of Christianity. His grandparents remember attending a public school where there were numerous Christian children. When the time came for lunch, the teacher asked the children to pray to God for food to appear. When they did, no food appeared. They were then asked to pray to "Father Stalin." Those who did were amazed to see a cart of food, fruits, nuts, and candy roll through the classroom door. This was repeated daily, brainwashing the children into believing that Stalin and the Communist regime were the sole providers of their food.

The youth living today are accepting radical ideologies that have totally failed. Multitudes who migrated to America from former Communist and Socialist nations are against both systems as they witnessed first-hand the oppression, government control, loss of freedoms, and hatred toward religion. Personal poverty, oppression, and a basic, simple life eventually rule in the majority of Socialist-Communist countries.

WHEN GOD CAME DOWN

All the Babel-Babylon cities are doomed for destruction. The original tower came crashing down, sending the people fleeing in confusion in all directions. Nebuchadnezzar's city of Babylon was overthrown during a one-night invasion by the Mede and Persian armies. The future megacity named "Mystery Babylon" is destroyed in one hour, perhaps engulfed by a nuclear holocaust (Rev. 18:10, 17, 19). The bricks of Babel cannot withstand God's judgment. Daniel saw the stone cut out of the mountain crash down upon the kingdoms of this world. The kingdom of stone, which is the Kingdom of God and Christ, will one day fill the earth, and all men will worship Christ, the King of Kings, in Jerusalem. That is when the New World Order will be removed and defeated by a Messianic Reset!

CHAPTER 2

PLANS FOR A GLOBAL RESET

When the pandemic shut down global travel and the world's business economy, and when the secular media, including social media giants, rejoiced with Joe Biden being in the White House, a new phrase was being written and reported publicly, "The New Global Reset." In the past, the same concepts presented in the Great Global Reset Manifesto were called "The New World Order" or "The Globalist Agenda." However, among knowledgeable conservatives, these older phrases were code words indicating the eventual loss of numerous freedoms that America has enjoyed, leading the nation like sheep to the slaughterhouse, causing Americans to submit to global rules and pay global taxes, allowing self-appointed rich elitists to rule over them. There is a movement to limit religious freedom by banning certain content in minister's messages, opposing any opinions that are opposite to the manifest of this new system. Progressives have learned that confiscating guns will lead to a revolt. Their plan is to control the sale and distribution of ammo. Without ammunition, a gun is useless.

In this reset, the Media Mongols and Tech Giants work in cooperation with the new global agenda. These companies stand to financially benefit as they control computers, search engines, and the information highway, being globally linked, controlling all news and propaganda in every nation. They see billions of dollars being made in a one-world government.

Modern progressives have learned that in order to present any controversial *ideology,* they must rename it or market it in a manner to make it publicly acceptable. In the past, those on the left were called "Liberals." Their name was changed to "Progressives." The mental concept is, if you don't think as a "progressive" does, you are a social dinosaur, stuck in traditional thinking, rejecting progressivism by not changing with the times. The word "socialism" has carried a negative connotation with many individuals who immigrated to America from Socialist nations whose economies are now in shambles. The new phrase became "social progressives." A third name change came with the term "Global warming," which was first alluded to in June 1988. Allegedly, the planet is warming, endangering massive ice burgs that are melting, raising water levels that will destroy all coastal areas. This warming is said to be creating dangerous holes in the ozone layer by carbon emissions. In fact, it was predicted that by now (2020), Florida's coastal cities would be partially underwater. In the 1990s, the Global Warming proponents warned that winters would be non-existent, as world temperatures were rising, changing the seasons from fall to spring, disregarding winter altogether. However, in the early 2000s, the world began to experience record-breaking cold and snow. A new term replaced Global Warming. We were introduced to the idea of "Climate Change." Thus, if it was too cold or too hot, this phrase was applied for either weather pattern. The phrase "One-World Government" is becoming "The Great Reset."

The idea of a Global Reset is called, by Hill News, "The most ambitious and radical plan the world has seen in more than a generation." The World Economic Forum met to discuss the need to "reset" the world economies after COVID. Instead of using traditional Capitalism, the group believes more Socialistic policies must replace the old economic system. This includes more regulations, an expensive New Green Deal, new wealth taxes, and other radical changes that must occur. The reset includes reforming the fossil fuel and gas industry. This move to change is directed by Prince Charles and Klaus Schwab. The United Nations, the International Monetary Fund, Microsoft, and other corporate leaders have attended reset discussions. According to the Hill article, those heading up the Great Reset must follow the policies of "American Socialists" such as Senators Bernie Sanders and Alexandria Ocasio-Cortez and initiate the multi-trillion-dollar New Green Deal. It was the economic shutdowns during the virus that served as the motivation for this new order. The main purpose behind this radical agenda is to save the planet due to Climate Change.

The directors of the Great Reset are activating radical and left-winged organizers to promote their plan, including training "climate Strikes" (protests) across the world. Prince Charles was quoted as saying, "The present pandemic is a golden opportunity for radical change."[1]

It is important to understand why the discussions of a Great Reset and Globalism are significant from a biblical worldview. Both Daniel and John, in their vision, reveal the major world empires (past and future) that have impacted or will impact Israel, Jerusalem, and the Jewish people. The previous biblical-prophetic empires that arose in world history are:

- The Egyptian Empire
- The Assyrian Empire
- The Babylonian Empire
- The Media-Persian Empire
- The Grecian Empire
- The Roman Empire

The Roman Empire, prophetically, is the most significant. The mighty Imperial Roman Empire began to split in AD 285 when Emperor Diocletian acknowledged that the Roman Empire had become too large to manage. He divided the Empire into two parts, the Eastern and the Western Roman Empires. The headquarters for the Western half remained in Rome, Italy, while the Eastern half selected Constantinople for their eastern base of operations. The Empire was permanently split in AD 395, never to rejoin as one empire. Continual invasions by pagan tribes slowly weakened the Western half. Eventually, Imperial Rome in the west became a memory in history, while Constantinople rose through economic success. Rome's final fall was in AD 476.

Eventually, Rome and Constantinople became strong *religious centers*, with the western half being the global headquarters for the Roman Catholic Church, ruled by cardinals and the Pope. The eastern half expanded into the Byzantine Empire, whose spiritual and political influence continued for nearly a thousand years, until May 28, 1453, when Constantinople fell to armies of the Islamic Ottoman Empire.

TWO PROPHETIC EMPIRES REMAINING

Based upon specific verses in the Apocalypse and secular history, six major prophetic empires have passed, with two remaining to be formed in the distant future. Biblically, these two have not been given a specific name but are identified with two numbers, the seventh and eighth. The biblical reference is alluded to in Revelation 17:10-11 AMPC:

> *"And they are also seven kings, five of whom have fallen, one still exists [and is reigning]; the other [the seventh] has not yet appeared, and when he does arrive, he must stay [but] a brief time. And as for the beast that [once] was, but now is no more, he [himself] is an eighth ruler (king, head), but he is of the seven and belongs to them, and he goes to perdition."*

The final eighth kingdom is a ten-nation or ten-king coalition aligned with the future Antichrist who will control the entire world for forty-two months (Rev. 13:15). When considering a future Global Government, this is where the seventh empire that will rule for a "short space" will emerge. This "short space" (KJV) refers to the first half of the seven-year tribulation, which lasts for forty-two months. It appears that the seventh kingdom will already be in existence at the time of Christ's return and will be the dominant system prior to the rise of the Antichrist's rule. Eventually, the Antichrist and his ten-king-nation confederacies invade Israel and Jerusalem, setting up their global headquarters (the eighth kingdom), operating militarily and economically from Jerusalem during the final three and one-half years of the tribulation.

Revelation 13 presents a sneak-peek into a future system in which this one-world dictator and his demonic-controlled team will seize complete global-economic control by forcing a new method of purchasing and selling through a three-part system, "a mark, a number, or a name" (Rev. 13:16-17). This scheme, known as the "Mark of the beast," is global, as we read, "He causes *all*, both small and great, rich and poor, free and bond to receive a mark in their right hand or in their foreheads" (Rev. 13:16).

The seventh empire is our focus. Daniel and John predicted that ten final kings and their nations would rule at the time of the Messiah's return. When the European Common Market was organized on March 25, 1957, with six nations uniting through a coal and steel trade emphasis, the pens-of-prophecy teachers went to work predicting this would be the ten-king organization. Then, in the 1980s, when 10 European nations joined the market, prophecy ministers began to theorize that these ten E.U. nations were the ten kings alluded to in Daniel 7:24 and Revelation 17:12. This joint-economic force became known in American prophetic circles as "The Revival of the Roman

Empire." Eventually, the ten nations expanded to more than 27. This fact changed some opinions toward the E.U. emerging to form the seventh empire. Others are suggesting these 27 nations will eventually be divided into ten regional groups, thus forming the ten kings.

The COVID pandemic impacted the economies in every nation, including the E.U. There were massive supply-chain disruptions, national closures of small businesses, a drop in oil prices, and a rise in precious metals. Trillions of dollars were printed and handed out to prevent an economic collapse. If another pandemic struck, the world's economies could fall into an abyss of chaos.

THE COVID RESET

The Great Reset focuses on five main progressive stages. The first is to remove and replace the dollar as the common global currency. The second strategy will be to initiate a cashless form of trade, used for both the selling and purchasing of products and services. This cashless system will eventually be a cyber or cryptocurrency. The cryptocurrency would be one that the reset system chooses or creates, under the approval of the Global Monetary Fund and World Banks. The third step is to diminish the influence and social impact of the traditional Christian religions, both Protestantism and Catholicism, by enforcing rules of punishment for intolerance. Messages no longer permitted are any that teach same-sex marriage is wrong, abortion should be overturned, or any that counter the culture. In some states, laws are being presented to make it illegal for a minister to counsel anyone in the gay lifestyle, establishing that it is "impossible" to change. The progressives pick and choose their moral beliefs. Some go as far as wanting to legalize prostitution, lower the age a teen can consent to sex, and legalize illegal drugs.

The fourth phase of this reset is to limit or control travel both domestically and internationally, using tracking chips, facial recognition, and other forms of A.I. technology. We have witnessed this with some airlines and nations, as they limit travel to anyone who has not taken the COVID vaccine. At this time, there are discussions that include everyone who travels across any state or national borders, or to and from a foreign nation, to have a special health chip implanted on their body, or have proof of being vaccinated by being a green passport carrier. It's amazing how the Passport is green, just as politicians speak of a Green New Deal. The fifth phase is to form a New Order where borders are removed, but all movement is controlled by tracking devices using special Passports or a special, personal identity chip.

To enact such drastic changes, the age-old concept of nationalism and American patriotism must be altered among America's citizens, which will never occur with the older generation who have experienced America's greatness. The strategy is that the children and grandchildren of the older generation must be reprogrammed in the public schools, colleges, and universities to accept the new order. To those resisting, they use social pressure, verbal and written forms, persecuting beliefs that are considered dangerous and outdated, possibly freezing the funds of conservative businesses.

Speaking of freezing funds to enact these radical and dangerous changes in a non-violent manner, the capability of these elitists, to prevent a person from accessing their money in their bank accounts, including canceling their credit cards and controlling their ability to sell products over the internet, has already been used to frighten others into submission. We have watched U.S. presidents sanction entire nations, freezing financial assets, preventing a dictator or terror group from withdrawing as much as one penny from their personal or national bank accounts. In 1973, Arab oil nations from the Gulf States voted to place an oil embargo against the United States for supporting

Israel during the 1973 Yom Kippur War. There was fuel rationing, high prices, and long gas lines, especially impacting large cities. This is also used as a weapon of retaliation.

With former President Trump's emphasis to "Make America Great Again," his four years disrupted the entire globalist agenda, as his goals included creating jobs, building new plants, providing tax breaks, and pressuring American based companies to return factories to the United States. For the first time, the Chinese Communists were held accountable in trade agreements. However, these wealthy globalists were impacted by the sanctions of China and set out to ensure Trump would never serve a second term. That was clear when certain directors and members of the F.B.I. and C.I.A. were presenting (later found to be found false) information to impeach Trump. The corruption also included high-level players in the Deep State Cabal. We must understand that the global progressives genuinely believe they have solo truth and are the self-appointed guardians to rescue precious mother earth from ecological destruction. The hundreds of millions of people connected to these ideas view traditional Christian theology as a by-gone relic. They would rejoice in seeing Bibles as just some books collecting dust under glass in the Smithsonian in Washington instead of being distributed in the hands of the people.

PREPARING FOR WHAT WAS TO COME

Eventually, all biblical prophecies related to the time of the end, including the numerous signs pointing to Christ's return, the tribulation judgments, and the alignment of the final world kingdoms, will all come to pass. According to a combination of scriptures, these events will merge during a period of time centered on seven years of great global distress. There will be one generation that will live to see the beginning of the end.

Imagine being a Jewish man, a husband with a large family, living in the bustling city of Jerusalem a few years prior to the invasion of Nebuchadnezzar's Babylonian army. Imagine hearing the controversial Hebrew prophet, Jeremiah, predict Jerusalem's utter destruction, also catching wind of other alleged "prophets" predicting that the Babylonian invasion would never come. You live in prosperity, hearing no reports of Babylonian troop movements by the Judean watchmen. As a family man, your main concern is farming, selling your produce at the markets, along with providing economic security and protection for your family.

Years later, you suddenly hear the sound of shofars echoing across the rugged Judean hills, signaling that a massive Babylonian army is marching across the Jordan Valley, eventually finding their way to Jerusalem. Days later, at sunrise, imagine seeing Jerusalem surrounded by thousands of armed men as fear and panic sweep over the city. Late one afternoon, you hear a mix of weeping and screaming, filling the air at the Temple as black pillars of smoke billow upward, darkening the blue sky. The stench of burning wood is suffocating everyone attempting to breathe fresh air. The white limestone floor at Solomon's Temple is covered with bodies and blood. For those who survive, knowing the words of Jeremiah, imagine yourself and your family taking that long march to your destiny, the pagan city of Babylon. Seventy years of Babylonian captivity had begun. Some who were older would die in Babylon and never see their Jewish homeland again.

What would you and your family have done? Scripture reveals that a few individuals, including the prophet Jeremiah, were permitted to remain in the land, along with a very small remnant. Other Jewish families had heard and believed the forty-year warnings of Jeremiah that complete destruction and captivity were coming. These discerning Jews had long departed the city, relocating to remote mountain areas, surviving the Babylonian destruction. The priest, false prophets, and the common people who mocked Jeremiah's warnings, to the point of threatening to kill him, were eventually chained and led from their Judean homeland to be prisoners in a strange land.

Similar patterns existed in Jerusalem before AD 70. Prior to the Roman Tenth Legion's invasion, Christ clearly revealed that both the Temple and Jerusalem would eventually fall to an invading army. In Matthew 23, Christ predicted that Jerusalem's desolation would occur within one generation, specifically, His. This indicated that it would happen within a forty-year period. History records how a few years prior to Jerusalem's final destruction, numerous Christians fled out of Jerusalem, making safe passage to the neighboring country of Jordan, where they formed a strong Christian community. Imagine knowing you were part of a generation that saw the fulfillment of major prophecies play out. It should be no surprise that we are a part of a prophetic generation.

I believe we have arrived at a time when many of the end-time biblical prophecies will be fulfilled. Some are positive in their fulfillment, and others are quite troubling. When the time comes for a global government, a universal tracking system, currency changes, and selective judgments, we must all learn how to be strong and take lessons from faithful believers in the past. They learned how to fast, pray, endure persecution, and remained true to the faith until the end.

America has been a glorious, free nation since 1776. It is a land where people from all tribes and nations dream of immigrating. Individual and national freedom is now and will be in the future, in danger of being slowly snuffed out. Just remember, some of you hearing this will be living when significant prophecies come to pass. It is not a curse to be alive at this time. It is a blessing to be a part of the end-time Revelation generation. Eventually, the kingdoms of this world will become the kingdoms of God (Rev. 11:15).

CHAPTER 3

CHRISTIANS FACING THE COURTS OF BABYLON

When the Tower of Babel collapsed, confusion struck the people, dividing them into different language groups. This was the beginning of the Table of Nations. Jewish rabbis teach that originally, there were seventy different divisions. This is because, after the flood, the Torah lists 70 descendants of Noah, as it is written, "These are the families (generations) of the sons of Noah" (Gen 10:1).[1] Centuries later, the plains of Shinar became known as Babylonia. Eventually, King Nebuchadnezzar constructed the city of Babylon, including his famous hanging gardens, one of the great wonders of antiquity.

It was Nebuchadnezzar who invaded Judea and Jerusalem, fulfilling Jeremiah's prophecy that the King of Babylon would march his armies into Judea and Jerusalem, taking Jewish captives back to Babylon for seventy years in exile. The Babylonians were idolatrous, worshipping and building elaborate temples to their gods. The Babylonian culture was the complete opposite of the devout Jews and their monotheistic beliefs.

After ruling over the Jews for seventy years, the Media and Persian armies overtook the Babylonians, annexing Babylon, making the massive city the seat of their new empire. The Persians were known for making laws that could never be broken. It wasn't long until Daniel was again in the "hot seat" for not following the laws of the land. He had visited this seat of controversy before.

DANIEL: A NON-COMPROMISER

Daniel's first test was in his teenage years when he and three male companions were being trained in the king's palace. They were selected above others for their physical appearance and wisdom. It appears they were being taught the customs and language of Babylon to be the go-betweens for the king's administration and the Jewish elders who only spoke Hebrew. The first test for these four young men, recorded in Daniel 1, was during a royal banquet, these devout Jews were offered meat sacrificed to idols, which was forbidden in the laws of the Torah. Daniel and his companions held strong to their convictions, rejecting the meat, instead, asking for ten days of lintels. If people in our current culture were living then, they would have "eaten what was set before them," taking the attitude, "When in Babylon, do what the Babylonians do." These four devout men of God would not compromise. In ten days, they looked better than the meat-eaters!

The second controversy is recorded in Daniel 6. A law was passed requiring that no person in the kingdom pray to any God for thirty days. If they were caught praying, they would be cast into a den of lions. This was a set up by Daniel's enemies to bring legal charges against him for praying and breaking this new law. Daniel ignored the law as he was unafraid of the death threat. He opened his window, faced Jerusalem, and prayed three times a day! He could have prayed in private and skipped the lion's den episode. His action was based on Solomon's instruction that if Israel went into captivity, they were to pray facing Jerusalem (1 Kings 8:47-48). This act was not in *defiance* of a law but in *obedience* to the highest law, a Divine order from God.

There comes a moment of decision when the higher law must outweigh man-made law if they run counter each other. In Acts 3, Peter and John healed a paraplegic, creating controversy among the religious Jews at the Temple. They confronted the Apostles with threats, saying they had to stop preaching and praying in the name of Jesus. These two Apostles boldly responded, "We ought to obey God rather than man" (Acts 5:29). Laws are to be obeyed until those laws are contrary to the spiritual, moral, and judicial instruction in the Divine Law of God. Daniel understood this.

The third test involved Daniel's three Jewish companions. Nebuchadnezzar constructed a large, gold idol. Some believe it was a replica of the metal image the king saw in a dream (Dan. 2) and may have been an image of the king himself. The king ordered that all people, without exception, bow and worship the image. When the music began blaring, the people began bowing — all except these three Hebrews. After being given several opportunities, these Jewish men were arrested and sentenced to death by burning in a large furnace. To the Babylonians, refusing a king's decree or rejecting to worship the national deity was a criminal offense. If this incident were in contemporary America, these three God-fearing men would be called "intolerant-radical-right-winged-religious fanatics." The newspaper headline would read, "Idol Phobia Exposed at Recent National Gathering." The secular media would have painted these devout religious Jews as "resisters and enemies of the state."

Two of these three narratives have one main theme: persecuting individuals who refuse to compromise their faith. Persecution has been an effective tactic used against an enemy from the earliest days.

THE LINE HAS BEEN DRAWN

There is a line in the sand. We are seeing a clash between the *ideology* of the bricks and the stones, which represents a struggle between two kingdoms, the kingdom of God and the kingdom of darkness. In Daniel's visions, there are two interesting forms of symbolism. Daniel indicates a final earthly kingdom formed by a ten-king confederation, which is symbolized on the metal image as "ten toes" consisting of a mix of "iron and clay" (Daniel 2). The interpretation is that the final government formed on earth, prior to Christ's return, will be "partly strong (the iron) and partly weak (the clay). In biblical times, the bricks were made from clay (or mud), which is the same substance God used to form Adam (Gen. 2:7). The final kingdom is built by human "bricks."

In the days of these ten kings, Daniel also observed a *stone* which was cut from a rock mountain, without the aid of men, crashing down on the metal image. The image (world empires) was broken into pieces, and the stone covered the entire earth. The stone is the Messiah, Jesus Christ, and His unshakable kingdom. Bricks are weak and can crack under extreme pressure. However, stones can endure heat and cold, ice and water, remaining in one spot, unmoved for a millennial. In Jerusalem, there are layers of large, white limestone ashlars, cut from ancient quarries that are over two-thousand years old. Although thousands of years old, most of these huge stones, making up the walls, look as if they were recently laid in place.

The kingdom of God is the "stone kingdom." God instructed Moses that when an altar was built, the stones were to be taken directly from the earth and not be "hewn," meaning no iron tool was to chisel and change their shape (Exod. 20:24-25). When we repent and enter the kingdom of God, the Almighty accepts us just as we are. When the Pharisees asked Christ to silence the crowds for their loud, exuberant worship, He replied to them, "If these should hold their peace, the stones (His people) would cry out" (Matt. 20:31). Christ also said:

> *"And think not to say within yourselves, We have Abraham to our father: for I say unto you, that God is able of these stones to raise up children unto Abraham."*
>
> – Matthew 3:9

Christ is represented by the stone Daniel saw, which is fitting because He is also called the "chief cornerstone" of the church (Eph. 2:20). As believers, I could use the idiom that we are "a chip off the old block."

THE GLOBAL BRICK-GOVERNMENTS

Those who are connected with the idea of forming a New World Order, or what others term a "Global Government," are the Nimrod's of modern Babel. They are planning for all of us to be reshaped as bricks, forming their system. They want to force the free people to adapt to their ultra-left ideologies, counter-culture fantasies, and anti-Christian biases. They are organizing a global network of clones and want the people to march in submission to their programs. If you resist becoming a global robot, a walking chipped computer, or combat your spiritual freedoms from being trampled; you will eventually be marked as an enemy of Babylon. The same God that quenched the violence of the Babylonian fiery furnaces and locked the jaws of the hungry lions when Daniel showed up is the same God that is still an enemy to the Babylonian spirit. Daniel's God is still superior. He demonstrated at Christ's tomb that He leaves no stone unturned.

In Babylon, the leaders took away the Hebrew names of their captives, giving them Babylonian names of idol gods. I noticed that

Daniel never used his "new" name but remained true to his Hebrew name. Christians are being tagged with lying names such as racists, homophobic, Islamophobic, and other false names, to mark us as something we are not. In these end-days, never allow the Babylonian system to redefine who you are as a Christian. You are a born-again son and daughter of the Most-High God, in covenant with His kingdom. The tower of Babel was created with bricks, but the kingdom of God is built with stones. Just as the tower fell, the kingdoms of men will falter, and the kingdom of God will rise in the earth. John predicted:

> *"Then the seventh angel sounded: And there were loud voices in heaven, saying, "The kingdoms of this world have become the kingdoms of our Lord and of His Christ, and He shall reign forever and ever!"*
>
> \- Revelation 11:15 NKJV

The "Stone" writing this book could not have said it any better.

CHAPTER 4

THE COMING PERSECUTION AGAINST CHRISTIANITY IN AMERICA

The dictionary definition of persecution is, "hostility and ill-treatment, especially because of race, political or religious beliefs."[1] Government persecution against religion is often unleashed progressively after marking specific targets. During the Roman Empire, opposition to the Gospel began with public disagreements between Jewish religious sects. Eventually, Christian bishops and pastors were being arrested for alleged "insurrections" instigated by religious agitators disagreeing with the preachers' messages. Arrest often led to punishments such as beatings. The worst result came when emotions raged, and laws were used to enforce the death penalty.

Prior to and after the American Revolution, public school teachers and Ivy League professors taught their students that the Pilgrims who journeyed on the Mayflower from England in 1620 set sail to America seeking *religious freedom* from oppression from the King and the Church of England. These were religious dissidents, united with the goal of forming a new colony based upon the Christian faith and personal freedom. Prior to the Pilgrims, in 1564, a group of French Protestants searching for religious freedom sailed from France, arriving in Florida. This colony was called the Huguenots. They formed a community at Fort Carolina near Jacksonville, Florida.

The Spanish arrived, establishing a base at Saint Augustine in Florida, eventually capturing and hanging all the Huguenots they found. Their reasoning was founded on the ideology that what the "heretics" were preaching (the doctrine of Luther) was contrary to the Catholic teachings of the Spanish. Our founders were intent on making the colonies a Christian-based union whose moral laws were based upon the laws in the Torah. Over time, America became a nation of immigrants that accepted all religious ideas, allowing freedom to express those beliefs without fear of oppression, arrests, or persecution.

This tolerance and acceptance of all beliefs, like a magnet, attracted many ethnic groups from oppressive nations. However, with the rise of non-religious progressives who believe they are lighthouses guiding the way to a new level of tolerance, Christians and their faith have been a target. They criticize, saying Christians "force" their beliefs upon others. Sometimes, specific biblical laws and rules given by the Almighty oppose certain beliefs taught by radical progressives, and that is the truth. God's word teaches that life begins in the womb, is sacred, and each tiny human has an eternal soul and spirit that will live forever. In true biblical teaching, to willingly take the life of a pre-destined human, of any age, in or out of the womb, is considered the sin of "shedding innocent blood." The clash over abortion has raged since 1973. The same is true with the biblical view of a marriage covenant. God created a woman in such an amazing way that if she is a virgin at marriage, upon consummating with her husband, she sheds a small amount of blood. In the sight of the Creator, this is a visible sign that she has entered a blood covenant with that one man, her husband.

Many progressives are heard mocking biblical marriage, saying it is ok to live together, have multiple sexual partners, and same-sex relations. When a Christian supports the biblical view, to intimidate them, the progressives will blog accusations on social media, falsely accusing the Christian of being homophobic, out of touch with reality, or a hatemonger.

The battle is not just with opposing beliefs, but whether opposing ideas should be suppressed "for the betterment of society." *One-sided freedom is actually partial bondage.* Throughout history, when violent, political, or religious persecution set itself against a righteous people and their causes, leading to arrests and death, the followers of truth began seeking a new place of refuge where they could survive and thrive far away from their oppressors. The question for Christians in America is, where will *we* go if, over time, on a state or federal level, they begin to shut down our voices, padlock our churches, and ban our Bibles? Which, by the way — using reformed hate crimes laws, they could eventually do.

THE GAME-CHANGER

When the messengers of righteousness are silenced, God will invoke a sudden game-changer. There are several game-changers revealed in Scripture. The first example is recorded in the story of Lot. This righteous man, living in the city of Sodom, was vexed every day with the wickedness he was seeing and hearing (2 Pet. 2:7-8). Lot was dwelling among hundreds of perverse men who never confronted or threatened Lot personally. However, one evening, when the old and young men surrounded Lot's house, they actually threatened to gang-rape him if he did not bring the two strangers he was protecting outside so they could molest them. The incident was as follows:

> *"And they said, "Stand back!" Then they said, "This one came in to stay here, and he keeps acting as a judge; now we will deal worse with you than with them." So they pressed hard against the man Lot, and came near to break down the door. But the men reached out their hands and pulled Lot into the house with them, and shut the door."*
>
> – Genesis 19:9-10 (NKJV)

When this violent mob attempted to break into Lot's home, physically threatening him, the two angelic messengers warned Lot to get out of town by sunrise because the Almighty had set the time for Sodom's destruction. Within twelve hours, the entire valley was engulfed in flames. Some people believe it was from a sudden underground explosion so strong, it sent fireballs into the atmosphere, raining the fiery sulfur and lava down on every building and consuming the people to ashes.[2] The threat and attempted violence against Lot and the two strangers (who were angels in the form of men—Heb. 13:2) removed any protective restraint that prevented the annihilation of four cities.

A second example can be found in the story of Jeremiah. King Zedekiah, who was under political pressure, threw the prophet Jeremiah into a dungeon filled with mud. The king burned Jeremiah's parchment describing, in detail, his written warnings. He permitted this mighty messenger to be persecuted and harassed by his own people. When the warnings of Jeremiah finally came to pass, the soldiers of Babylon plucked out the king's eyes and led him into Babylon bound in chains. However, Jeremiah escaped the captivity and was given freedom by the Babylonians to remain in the land. In a third example, King Ahab hired prophets to tell him only what he wanted to hear. One true prophet, whose predictions the king hated, was banished to a dungeon, preventing anyone from hearing his messages of "doom and gloom."

These "kings" were in sole control of the national propaganda. Everyone was forced to take the bait, "hook, line, and sinker," and were too filled with intimidation to express any opposing view. Today, our "kings" are the media-elites sitting in their planning centers, determining who to exalt publicly and who to erase, making them appear irrelevant. This selective-approval or disapproval sounds just like the social media giants who pick and choose what will be censored and what will be permitted. *They sterilize content faster than a surgeon preparing for major surgery.*

Four hundred false prophets told Ahab to go to battle. One true prophet, Micaiah, warned Ahab he would die in battle. A false prophet named Zedekiah struck Micaiah on the cheek accusing him of a false prediction. The following day, Ahab was killed in battle, and the false prophet Zedekiah went into hiding (1 Kings 22). Stories in the New Testament, especially the book of Acts, indicate how God Himself will suddenly rise up to judge a leader who mistreats and persecutes His covenant people. Pharaoh, the King of Egypt, controlled the persecution, but God controlled the plagues. The persecuted later danced on the other side of the sea, while Pharaoh sunk like a stone to the bottom of the ocean becoming, shark food.

NATIONAL SAFE HAVENS

Throughout Scripture, when persecution arose in one region, those who were forewarned or discerned the times often prepared plans to relocate. Examples include:

- When a famine was decimating Canaan, Jacob and his entire family *relocated* to Goshen in Egypt, where they thrived for decades, growing into a strong nation of 600,000 men (Exod. 12:37).

- In the time of King Saul, for thirteen years, David was hunted by Saul and his soldiers from cave to cave. Instead of making himself an open target by hanging around Saul's palace, David surrounded himself with 600 men of war, going "underground" throughout the *Judean Wilderness* and Southern Israel for many years until Saul's death.

- The prophet Elijah was under a death threat from Queen Jezebel. Instead of sitting at the gates of Jezreel, waiting for the angry queen to retaliate and behead him, the prophet traveled nearly 280 miles to spend time alone in a cave. It would have been unwise for this prophet who was wanted dead or alive to remain anywhere near Jezebel and her henchmen.

- In the New Testament, When Herod heard of the Messiah's birth, he assigned a military regiment with orders to kill any infant under two years of age. After an angelic warning in a dream, Joseph, Mary, and the Christ child immediately fled from Bethlehem, journeying to Egypt, remaining there until Herod's death (Matt. 2:16-23). The holy family left the danger zone for a more peaceful location, later returning and living in Nazareth.

- In Luke 1, John the Baptist's father, Zacharias, served as a priest in Jerusalem at the temple. However, John was a wild prophet who, instead of wearing white robes, sported a camel-hair garment held together with a leather belt, eating wild honey and locusts. He certainly didn't fit the concept of a traditional Jewish priest's son. To hear him speak, people had to leave their cities and towns, travel to the desolate Judean Wilderness, sit on the banks of the Jordan River—in the middle of nowhere—to watch a baptismal service and hear this desert prophet teach.

- One of the most noted *exodus* accounts, often overlooked, is the warnings Christ gave to His followers, predicting that Jerusalem would be destroyed within one generation (Matt. 23:34-38). The main sign indicating destruction would soon occur was when Roman armies were surrounding the city and digging a trench:

"*For days will come upon you when your enemies will build an embankment around you, surround you and close you in on every side, and level you, and your children within you, to the ground; and they will not leave in you one stone upon another, because you did not know the time of your visitation.*"

– Luke 19:43-44 (NKJV)

In the year AD 66, devout Christians living in Judea and Jerusalem saw military conflicts between the Roman soldiers and rebellious Jewish militias. Christians observed Roman soldiers constructing encampments for their legions. That was the prophetic trigger motivating many Christians to pack what they could and depart out of the area to escape the coming desolation. They remembered the instructions of Christ, "Let him who is in Judea, flee to the mountains" (Matt. 24:16). Many Christians escaped from Jerusalem prior to the Roman Tenth Legion, slaying thousands of Jews at the sacred temple, later setting it on fire. The Christians were directed by an angelic revelation to flee to Pella, a city built in Jordan that gave Christians asylum and freedom to settle in the region and build a Christian community. Many Jewish zealots, up until the final moments, believed that God would intervene and alter the outcome of the war, supernaturally delivering His people from the danger of the Roman military. Two opposing beliefs emerged. Those who heard recalled and followed Christ's forty-year-old prophetic warnings to get out, and others who held to a false hope, whose fighting proved useless, as the divine prophecies were contrary to their false expectations. The point is, in each case, there was a safe haven during the crisis.

SAFE STATES AND UNSAFE STATES

It is not a question of *if*, but of *when* various forms of persecution against Christians and true patriots will begin in the United States. The big question is, can it be defeated by a national, peaceful resistance of patriots and Christians, or will the extremists with Marxist, Socialist, and Fascist ideology seize control in every area, leading to future arrests of believers? Peaceful protests include flooding your Senators and Congressmen and women with protest letters, demanding they resist the dangerous trends and abominable laws. This strategy includes boycotting stores and products that support the agendas we do not support. Christians must find and use alternative social media platforms and reject those banning conservative and Christian free speech. It also involves helping register millions of Christians who have never voted so they can vote. Only by being active in these methods of peaceful resistance will anything change.

In 2012, when the owner of Chick-fil-A made a public statement favoring traditional marriage, the gay community called a national boycott to bring the company down financially. In response, Christians came together, and the lines to order food across America were so long that many of the Chick-fil-A stores ran out of food. It was the biggest financial day in Chick-fil-A history, and the restaurant chain has survived and prospered. We should support any business whose owners align with biblical principles.

While some say a total shutdown of religions and personal freedoms could never occur in the United States, just remember, the Russian Tzars never realized the impact of the Communist revolution until they were removed. The German people were deceived into thinking Hitler would be a positive leader. In our nation, oppressive and freedom-killing legislation would be the method used to chain targeted groups to the pillar of silence and irrelevance.

The United States was set up with the separation of powers to ensure one body would not be in complete control. The "balance of power" is split between the Judicial, Legislative, and Executive branches. The Legislative branch makes the laws, the Executive branch carries out the law, and the Judicial branch evaluates the laws. There is also a flow to the order. We have a Federal Government, State Governments, and Local (county and city) Governments. The main leaders are the president (federal), the governor (state), and the mayor (local or county). Throughout history, there have been times when the state and federal government clashed, causing a great rift in the nation. This clash is what initiated the Civil War.

Since the time of the Civil War, there has been a moral-social-religious division in the United States. In the northeastern part of the U.S. (and the West Coast), the majority of voters are Democrats, including a mix of radical Progressives, radical Socialists, Leftists, and Marxists. The Southern states and Midwest lean more conservative. These states, known in 2020 as the "red states," recognize the three Gs: God, guns, and old glory (the U.S. flag).

For years, the progressives have openly mocked and rebuked the Christians for being narrow-minded racists and bigots who are intolerant of other viewpoints. We were informed by the secular media how "open-minded" and "tolerant" the liberals are, creating a false impression that their tolerance works both ways. Their "open-mindedness is a two-headed coin. They flip it calling heads, and win every time.

We have also seen how this "open-minded" and "tolerant" theory only works if you accept, cooperate, and push their agenda. We saw in early 2021 just how *open-minded* such tolerant thinkers they were when the tech giants began taking down various conservative and some religious videos that were contrary to their personal, political agendas. Perhaps it is possible to be so "opened-minded" that all of your common-sense falls out!

THE STATES RIGHTS

In 1869, before the Civil war, the southern states had an estimated 42,000 plantations with up to 4 million African slaves. The southern plantations depended upon mass agricultural production, including cotton, tobacco, sugar cane, and spices. Most plantation owners were affluent. One reason so many plantations existed in the southern states was due to the good soil for planting.[3]

Cotton and other products were planted and sold in America, but the majority of our income was through exports to Europe. America's northern states were economically more industrial in nature, and northern industries were growing, requiring additional revenue secured by raising state or federal taxes, helping pay for the growth of new factories in the large northeastern cities.

While this explanation may be simplified, disagreements on taxes, tariffs, states' rights, and the future of slavery came to a boiling point between the northern and southern politicians, governors, and people. "States' Rights" refers to the struggle between individual states and the Federal Government. Southern states joined together in protests as they felt their rights were being infringed upon by those in the northern states, believing they had no right to impose through their congressmen in Washington, influencing the laws and taxes they had to pay, benefiting one side. The real battle was over slavery, which, at the time, the northern states were against and favored by the majority of the southern states.

The idea of states' rights, as viewed by southern states, was that the states were supreme as the government in Washington had been created by the states, including the thirteen original colonial states. To many southern states, certain national laws did not necessarily apply to them, allowing each state to determine which federal laws they should or should not follow. We see this same controversy in 1787 when the Constitution was being debated for fear that a national government could threaten each states' sovereignty and independent liberties. It was Jefferson who, almost *prophetically*, warned that certain Acts passed into federal law could eventually be used by the national government to restrict freedom of speech.

In December of 1860, South Carolina voted to succeed from the United States. Other southern states soon followed. To prevent the United States from being divided into two nations with two capitals and two presidents, the Civil War befell the nation. While the central issue was certainly slavery, there was also a mix of taxes, tariffs, and states' rights that clashed with the national government.

As tensions grew, South Carolina and Mississippi called for secession. Eventually, 11 southern states united together, forming the Confederate States of America. In 1861, these 11 states chose their own president, Jefferson Davis, and selected a new Confederation capital, Richmond, Virginia. Soon thereafter, Richmond was filled with 1,000 government members, 7,000 civil servants, and countless Confederate troops waiting for the battle to begin.

Over 150 years later and we are still in a battle of rights, only it's a new one. The power of the individual states cannot exceed that of the Federal Government, meaning a state cannot pass or impose any law that is in violation of federal law. Certain rights exist in which limited power is given to the states as long as a law passed is not contrary to the Constitution. States do have the power to pass their own legislation as it relates to state matters such as raising state taxes, property laws, and other basic needs. The main reasons for forming the Federal Government were demonstrated when the thirteen colonies (all independent) realized, during the Revolutionary War, their need for a centralized government. The Federal Government was necessary to form and oversee a united military and to determine war and peace. The President and Congress are involved in world trade agreements and other important national obligations. The fear that laws restricting gun ownership, the sale of ammo, the right of free speech, freedom of religion, and the restriction of information, is creating another division between the South and the North.

RED VERSUS BLUE

The Civil War soldiers were known for their colors of blue and grey, blue represented the Union troops, and grey represented the Confederate troops. Thankfully, today, no weapons are being fired, but there is a growing animosity and distrust between the more conservative *red* states and the liberal *blue* states. With 24-hour cable news, 24-hour satellite news, and internet news, viewers cringe when hearing verbal lashings between the two opposing ideologies. Both sides demonize the ideologies of the other.

Many of the ultra-liberal states have such oppressive business regulations and high taxes that people are moving, by the tens of thousands, out of those states (especially the West Coast) to more moderate or conservative states. They are weary and exhausted of governors and mayors controlling their personal lives and piling on new taxes when during the COVID shutdowns, many went through months without work. Others are also disgusted with violent protests, the legalizing of dangerous drugs, and roaming mobs of youth attacking innocent bystanders on the streets. They have packed up and moved from the shadows of Sodom and Gomorrah to a little town like Zoar, as Lot and his daughters did (Gen. 19).

Wise families are researching, picking and choosing new locations in which to live. For example, a few years back, the state of Tennessee was 12 in overall ranking among states where individuals and families were moving. It was recently raised to the number one state people are moving to, ranking slightly above Texas, with East Tennessee being a primary destination. One U-Haul company's president in Nashville said, "I'm seeing a lot of people from California move (to Tennessee) because they're attracted to our lifestyle." He added, "Tennessee has no income tax and is very business friendly."[4] Tennessee is generally a conservative state with 11,542 recognized churches. In Tennessee, surveys indicate that 81 percent of Tennesseans profess to be *Christians.*[5] Many people view Tennessee, Southwestern Virginia, Kentucky, West Virginia, and states in the "Deep South" as "Pro-Constitutional States" with "cities of refuge" not bent on restricting religious or personal freedoms.

Another interesting fact about Tennessee is the results of a poll that was taken listing the top 25 "Most Bible Minded" cities in the United States. Three of the top ten were located in Tennessee: Knoxville, Chattanooga, and Tri-Cities. Chattanooga is located 20 miles from my home and was listed as number one, with 50% of the population believing in the Bible.[6]

There are other liberal states in which the city mayors and state governors pass laws or rules, making it difficult for a Christian church to purchase property, including many challenging regulations that stifle Christian-based building programs. Some cities pass sub-division restrictions, limiting the number of people allowed in a small group-home Bible study. In comparison, in our hometown of Cleveland, Tennessee, in the past, there have been Bible study groups that meet before and after school, prayer that is offered at ball games, and freedom to have large meetings and even outdoor religious gatherings. Our town is about forty miles from the North Carolina mountains, where the first major outpouring of the Spirit occurred in 1898. Cleveland has a large Christian university, a Theological school, the I.S.O.W. internet Bible school, and our county, Bradly County, is blessed with 115 strong churches along with numerous other congregations. I have heard that the entire county houses over 300 churches (a few are older country churches that have closed down).

Many who come to the southeastern mountains purchase property for farming or just to retire, enjoying the feeling of safety they sense, having good, hard-working people as neighbors that share similar spiritual and political beliefs. In Scripture, there were six major cities of refuge that a man could flee to for protection if he accidentally slew another man until an investigation was held. I believe there are numerous states within the United States whose people and elected officials will be found standing up, resisting oppressive laws, as much as possible, to maintain all forms of freedom we have enjoyed.

Throughout America's history, most wars we have been involved in are in some way connected to receiving or holding on to freedom. For the Colonists, the Revolutionary War was necessary to liberate the colonies from the control of the British monarchy. The Revolution was a revolt, a fight for independence and freedom. The Civil War was a struggle for men and women to be liberated from slavery. The battle theme was freedom. The World Wars, especially World War II, united the allies to stop the Jewish holocaust by defeating, then destroying the Nazi regime, freeing Western Europe and the world from a dangerous, mentally unstable dictator. The 1991 Gulf War was to remove the "butcher from Baghdad," Saddam Hussein, from power, liberating Iraqis from their radical Muslim dictator.

The Marines, Army, Navy, National Guard, and Special Ops have defended America from enemies both foreign and domestic. From 1775 to 2010, millions of American soldiers have died in wars, fighting for freedom while defending it.

Will the blood of millions of soldiers reach the ears of the Almighty in His heavenly temple in the same manner that Abel's blood cried from the ground for vengeance (Gen. 4:10) if America's national government, with its new socialist politicians, begin a campaign using the old playbook of the Marxists or Fascists, banning free expression, telling ministers what they cannot say, stopping our second amendment rights? Will hundreds of years of the thundering of cannons, the clashing of swords, the deafening sound of explosions, and coffins wrapped in American flags honored by a 21-gun salute all be in vain?

You and I will decide. The questions to answer are, "Who is on the Lord's side?" and "Who wants to remain free?"

CHAPTER 5

SHOULD CHRISTIANS RESIST OR SUBMIT TO A CORRUPT GOVERNMENT?

By AD 70, the Christian faith had struck the earth like an unseen meteorite from space, making its initial impact in Jerusalem then spreading shockwaves throughout the Roman Empire. Within forty years, no Roman or Greek city had been left untouched by the Gospel message. In AD 54, with the rise of the evil dictator, Emperor Nero, Christianity was eventually targeted, with violent persecution, as a dangerous "cult." In Rome, Nero beheaded the Apostle Peter in AD 64 and the Apostle Paul in AD 65. There are several primary reasons why the Roman governmental leadership in the Empire, including emperors, governors, and procurators, resisted the spread of Christianity by using harassment, arrests, and legal trials.

SELECTIVE TOLERANCE

The Roman Empire was tolerant of any religion, especially the gods and goddesses of the Greeks. This is not just because the Romans were worshippers of different gods. Their tolerance was financially motivated. The empire collected taxes from tens of thousands of pilgrims generated by pilgrimages to the temples of Apollo, Diana, Zeus, and countless others. The city marketplaces located near these temples sold food, wines, miniature idols, meat for sacrifices, along with temple trinkets, providing coinage and economic stability to the cities and taxes for Roman coffers. Paul, Peter, and John's preaching led to conversions and began impacting the sales of small silver shrines being sold to idol worshippers (Acts 19:24-35). Following a great revival in Samaria, tens of thousands of dollars of occult scrolls and materials were collected and burned in a bonfire (Acts 19:19). When pagan worshippers converted to Christianity, the income to the local temples, shrines, and idol manufacturers drastically decreased, which in turn impacted Rome's tax revenue. To stop the financial bleeding, persecution and jail time often followed major apostolic-evangelistic meetings. To Roman authorities, *cash* was more important than *conversions,* and *taxes* were needed more than healing *testimonies.*

Christians vehemently rejected Roman emperor worship. Nero believed he was a god and deserved worship. Previous and future Roman emperors considered themselves earthly gods. Caesar Augustus, the Emperor at Christ's birth, was labeled "king of kings." From 31 BC to AD 68, cities throughout Asia Minor erected elaborate temples dedicated to the worship of Roman emperors. Rituals included animal sacrifices made on behalf of the emperor mixed with other offerings burnt to idols. In the New Testament, devout Jews refused to eat any "meat sacrificed to idols" (1 Cor. 8:10-13).

Some Christians and religious Jews refused to purchase the meat featured in the public markets of Asia Minor, fomenting another mini-economic shortfall. Christians were proclaiming the message of a new Kingdom that was now on earth (the Kingdom of God), creating the threatening perception that Christians would eventually overthrow Rome to establish their own earthly kingdom. Instead of worshipping human emperors, Christians worshipped the Son of God, Jesus the

Christ, whom they considered the only "King of Kings" (1 Tim. 6:15). This enraged the emperors and Roman authorities. During the latter centuries in the Roman empire, wicked emperors demanded worship from Christians under the threat of arrest or, at times, death. Christian historians note that some Christians forsook their faith to spare their own lives.

WEAPONLESS BELIEVERS

Christians were taught that their struggles were not with flesh and blood (people) but with spirit rebels operating throughout Satan's dark kingdom. Their sword was the word of God, and their armor was spiritual and invisible, according to Ephesians 6:12-18. Having studied the Roman Empire and early church history, I noted how passive Christians were when it came to accepting whatever persecution came their way. This is because Christians were taught not to be violent or shed innocent blood, focusing intently on Christ's love for their enemies. When they were arrested, there was little resistance. Prayer was their only weapon. A good example is when Herod arrested Peter, Christians in Judea organized an all-night home prayer meeting, intently interceding for Peter's safety and release. Christians also understood that to verbally or physically confront any Roman soldier could mean sudden arrest followed by jail time. This is why Jesus taught to "agree with your adversary quickly" and "if they ask for your coat, give them your cloak." He taught that if they ask you to go one mile, go two (Matt. 5:25, 40). These simple instructions seem quite passive, yet following them could save a person from serious conflict with Roman authorities. Romans would not allow resistance to their authority from any non-Roman. If Roman soldiers came upon a Jewish farm and wanted grain, the Jewish farmer provided it, or they should be prepared for soldiers to retaliate.

Christ taught us to be *spiritually* aggressive but said little or nothing about being *politically* aggressive. He taught that the "kingdom of heaven suffers violence and the violent take it by force" (Matt. 11:12). The end-time battle for a believer is to gain faith and hold on to it. When Christ was arrested, He told His disciples that upon His request, twelve legions (72,000) of angels could be released from His Father in heaven to fight for Him (Matt. 26:53). These angels were heaven's "secret service," God's protective messengers, angels on standby, ready to execute a plan to extract Christ from the earth.

Prior to Christ's major intercession in the Garden of Gethsemane, He suggested that Peter carry a sword. Christ knew that hundreds of men were coming to arrest Him, and one man with one sword could never slay 600 armed men. This was not Christ's intent for Peter's weapon. It was to test Peter's words when he said he would go with Christ even to death (Luke 22:33). Peter was a bit hasty at times but wasn't as "unwise" as some suggest. When he swung his sword, he never struck an armed Roman soldier. He struck an unarmed servant of the high priest named Malchus, who was very low on the totem pole of authority. Being a Jew, striking an armed soldier with a sword could bring instant death (at the worst) or arrest with jail time (at the least).

When dealing with governments, including corrupt laws or lawmakers, a believer must be "wise as a serpent and harmless as a dove," exercising wisdom, discretion, and self-control. For example, in 2021, those who broke windows while storming the Capitol should have studied the law before making such a decision based on mob emotion. Destroying federal property is a federal crime. Those who attended the rally and stayed clear of the assault were wise as serpents, harmless as doves, while those stealing property ended up with an extended "jail ministry."

PAUL AND THE ROMAN EMPIRE

Paul was Jewish but he was also a Roman citizen. After he was arrested and beaten, he told his punishers he was a Roman citizen, striking them with instant fear as a Roman could not be beaten as punishment without a fair trial. Paul knew the laws of Rome, the traditions of the Jews and knew how to use them for his benefit. During one arrest and trial, he eventually appealed to Caesar (which is like an appeal to the U.S. Supreme Court). He was granted permission for a legal hearing before the emperor.

Paul understood that governmental authorities could make life peaceful or difficult for Christians. He also knew that prayer had the potential to change negative outcomes and possibly a leader's heart. Paul knew this as he himself had received a life-altering conversion. He wrote:

> *"I exhort therefore, that, first of all, supplications, prayers, intercessions, and giving of thanks, be made for all men; For kings, and for all that are in authority; that we may lead a quiet and peaceable life in all godliness and honesty."*
>
> – 1 Timothy 2:1-2

The reason for this exhortation is that at the very time Paul penned this instruction from Rome, there was an early Jewish uprising being planned against the Roman soldiers by militias in Judea and Jerusalem. This anti-Roman occupation movement was expanding, eventually climaxing with the Great Jewish Revolt in AD 66 to AD 73. The rebellion began as an anti-taxation protest. The Roman governor plundered money from the Jewish Temple, then began arresting Jewish leaders. The continual violent attacks by the Jewish militia were called seditions. Eventually, the climax of the revolt ended for good with the Roman Tenth Legion's destruction of Jerusalem and the Second Temple. The sacred vessels of gold and silver were seized by the soldiers and carried by ship to Rome.

I am certain that Paul saw this political clash coming between Rome and the Jewish zealots and knew the conclusion would be death to all rebels and Jewish people. Christ had already predicted the destruction of Jerusalem as recorded in Matthew chapters 23 and 24. The outcome of this struggle would be similar to all of the Militia movements in the United States, attempting to fight face to face with a well-armed, well-trained United States military. We already know who would win.

With the obvious changes in America, turning from a freedom-oriented democracy to a Socialist-style rule, those who have studied history are noting the same parallels to the events in 1933, when Hitler was elected the Chancellor of Germany. Below I will reveal patterns found in comments that have been made on American media outlets, editorials in papers, news articles, and text messages made public.

IN GERMANY 1933-1939	IN THE UNITED STATES (AFTER 2020)
Hitler ran on a Democratic Socialist Platform	Socialist Democrats were Elected in 2020
The Nazi's controlled the propaganda for the Reich	The Secular Media are the liberals' mouthpieces
The German media silenced opposing voices	Tech giants banned conservative voices
The Germans prepared concentration camps	Liberals speak of "reprogramming camps"

The Germans began arresting protesters	The government began arresting protesters
Many German-Christians supported Hitler at first	Many Christians are supporting Socialism
The Jews were targeted as enemies of the state	Christians and patriots are targeted as enemies

I heard Lester Sumrall, a powerful minister, relate that when he was a young man, he was speaking in Germany at the same time that Hitler was running for Chancellor. During a night service, the pastor of a Protestant church informed Lester that the offering that night would be going to support Hitler. The future dictator had used media propaganda, announcing the Christians and churches in Germany supporting him would be recognized and favored in his administration. At that time, most had no clue of the death, carnage, and destruction of the Jewish people and the world that Hitler would initiate six years later.

THE CHURCH AND UPRISINGS

Solomon wrote, "There is a time of war and a time of peace" (Eccl. 3:8). Prior to and during America's Revolutionary War, a sharp division of opinions swept through the colony's churches. Among the Anglican priests, the clergy made vows "before God and man" to be loyal to the king and to the Church of England. Other ministers, such as Jonathan Mayhew, pastor of the West Church in Boston, taught that fighting the tyrant British who occupied the colonies was the duty of Christians. When the war began, over half of the Anglican priests gave up their ministry instead of breaking the vow to the king.[1] The Quakers, who were pacifist, were also divided, with many resisting engaging in a military-style campaign. Some devout Christians viewed participation in war as taking the life of another human, which they believed broke the Commandment, "Thou shalt not kill" (Exod. 20:13).

Other Protestant ministers in the colonies began viewing the struggle for American independence as a righteous cause worthy of being sanctioned by the church and Christians. Some ministers served as military chaplains, members of the legislators, or Congress. Newspaper print spread the news of ministers supporting the war. Sermons became mingled with gospel messages and political opinions favoring the Revolution.

Ministers in the colonies, just as prophetic ministers often do, explored stories in the Bible, discovering parallels concealed in important biblical events. During the American Revolution, a painting called *The Hanging of Absalom,* created by Robison Trumbull (1718-1780), shows Absalom hanging from a tree while King David plays a harp above the tree and the general who hung Absalom (Joab in the Bible) is standing below him. The depiction is to illustrate that Absalom was a patriot, similar to the colonists, resisting the tyrant rule of his father David, who in this case represented King George III, and in the painting, Joab is depicted as a red coat.[2] When America received independence, several founders viewed it as the children of Israel being delivered from Pharaoh, marching toward their Promised Land, which was America. One of the early ideas for America's national seal was an image of Israel crossing the sea as Pharaoh's army drowned with the caption, "Death to Tyrants."

America's Revolutionary War for independence was a violent uprising with 6,800 colonists killed in action, 6,100 wounded, and over 20,000 taken prisoner. There were an estimated 17,000 deaths attributed to disease. The cost was staggering, including the loss of homes, businesses, livestock, and personal possessions.[3] The war came with great costs, as the United States spent $400 million in wages to its troops. The Revolutionary War demonstrated the unquenchable desire men have to be free from government tyranny and oppression, exposing the price men will pay to be free from religious and political suppression.

THE CIVIL RIGHTS MOVEMENT

The American Revolution created three Charters of Freedom and Liberty that we have enjoyed since 1776, the Declaration of Independence, finalized in 1776, the Constitution, ratified in 1788, and the Bill of Rights, completed in 1791. The Federalist Papers, written from 1787-1788, were compiled to detail how the American government might operate. One line in the Declaration of Independence states that "All men are created equal." This became the motivating theme for a major non-violent uprising that would change civil-right laws in America.

The Civil Rights movement was a decades-long struggle that reached a climax in 1964, one hundred years after the abolishing of slavery. The blacks were being discriminated against on buses, in restrooms, restaurants, and were segregated in schools, especially in the south. The primary voice of the Civil Rights Movement was a Baptist minister from Montgomery, Alabama, Martin Luther King, Jr. Using boycotts, marches, massive rallies, Freedom Riders, and the power of public speaking, over a period of several years, state and federal laws were changed, or new laws made. King and his followers proved that laws could be changed when the masses came together as one, and the changes could be done without bullets and guns.

For several years, new forms of protests have emerged, with many beginning peaceful then turning violent. Some had pre-planned violence, including looting, burning cars, businesses, and bringing economic pain and division within the communities.

THE LOSS OF FREEDOM

In the month of January 2021, when the MAGA Trump march in Washington, D.C. ended with a forced break-in at the U.S. Capitol, the media and talking heads of journalists interviewing so-called experts in political science began to express their *real* views, not just toward a few hundred instigators, but toward anyone and everyone who was conservative, and especially any Trump supporter.

They made it clear that everyone, including all of the 75 million people who voted for Trump, needed to be forced to undergo "reprogramming" in a special government-sponsored camp. These same types of camps are used in China to "assist" (actually force) a person in changing their beliefs. In this case, these camps could be used to establish conservative ideology as wrong. One person suggested organizing special camps to force "these people" to undergo evaluations. One progressive publicly said it would be acceptable to separate parents from their children if need be. The radical left began saying that those in the House and Senate who believed there was voter fraud should resign, or at least be put on a no-fly list, which is a penalty for anyone being labeled a possible domestic terrorist. This is pure Marxist-style harassment.

After January 6, 2021, rumors began spreading across the internet that the Trump legal team was preparing to release documents, pictures, and eyewitness evidence of voter fraud directly to the American people after weeks of being rejected by state legislators, state courts, and the Supreme Court. Immediately, all major social media platforms banned Trump and his entire team, preventing them from releasing any possible documentation directly to the American people. The House and Senate both rejected the idea of conducting a ten-day audit on the vote in the controversial battle-ground states, leaving an estimated 75 million people feeling fed-up that their own elected legislators were themselves corrupt and co-conspirators in a coverup.

Radical leftists admit their admiration for the radical ideologies of Marxism and Democratic-Socialism. Marxism is the baby of Communism and a form of Democratic-Socialism that molded the manifesto for German Fascism under Hitler. When do we, who love religious freedom and free speech, say, "Enough is enough?" and how can anyone drain a swamp with more *alligators* than there is *water*?

Corruptors protect their corruption and power. During the entire length of the Roman Empire, including the persecution against Christians by ten different emperors, individual Christians either became bold and unmovable or weak and washy in their faith. They never initiated violent protests but went underground, as evidenced when seeing thousands of tombs in the Roman Catacombs. They were pacifists toward violence, praying for their enemies prior to suffering martyrdom. Today, if we silence our voices, lay down our pens, and hide behind our four walls, this is viewed by our enemies as passivity and weakness and is a sign they have won without a fight. Before Christ's return, *America must lay down more freedom-concrete to strengthen the cracking foundations being beaten by the hammers of intolerance toward our religious freedom.* If our freedom collapses, the rest of the world will follow. Since the Gospel must be preached to all nations of the world before Christ can return (Matthew 24:14), we can say true Bible believers have God on our side, and He will ensure His church can and will speak His message to the nations!

Discerning patriotic Americans, especially biblically literate Christians, must learn the secrets of survival from men and women who have lived under Communist and Socialist governments that suppress human freedom, control what is and is not to be written on the printed page, along with silencing free speech, allowing and promoting religious persecution. This persecution is often dished out by governments being led by atheists, dictators, and even fanatics. How do people who crave freedom but live under iron-fisted repression operate, communicate, and survive? My trips into former Communist nations and information from those who travel secretly in dangerous Islamic places have taught me lessons that must be learned in the West.

As freedom-loving free people, we must never submit to an evil diabolical system led by tyrants but must learn to out-pray, out-think, out-smart, and out-strategize them. At times, when Christ was threatened, instead of choosing confrontation, He would slip out and secretly move away from the area of danger, going into seclusion in a desert for a season, reappearing in a different location. Elijah did the same. When Ahab sought out Elijah at his normal location, he was gone. The prophet went from caves to mountains, including crossing the border to other nations during times of persecution.

How should we pray for an evil government? We cannot pray a "blessing" on what God does not bless, nor favor upon what God Himself disfavors. We must keep in mind that God alone controls the blessing and the curse on a people or a nation.

We should first pray for the salvation of their soul, including God removing their hearts of stone. We should ask the Almighty to begin to open the eyes of their understanding and for God to reveal Christ to them. We should also agree that any law opposing God's higher-law and any legislation that would silence the voices of God's men and women would utterly fail.

The United States has arrived at a season in its history in which Christians and freedom seekers should begin studying the various methods used by Christians in extreme Socialist and Communist nations and the methods they used to survive and continue their work. We may need to follow their steps in the future. See Chapter 8 on "The Strategies of Oppressed People."

CHAPTER 6

THE BALAAM PLOT AND AMERICA'S SELF-CURSE

Several years ago, I was researching the impact of the blessings and the curses of the law listed in Deuteronomy 28. Obedience releases an increase in family and finances, while a curse does just the opposite. I came across a significant story, recorded in Numbers chapters 22 through 24, that exposes a level of Satanic strategy that has gone undetected within the Body of Christ. It exposes a specific strategy that the adversary is effectively using against the entire United States, without their knowledge.

In the story, Israel had departed from Egypt, crossed the Red Sea, and was encamped in a valley in the land of Moab. There were between 1.5 to 2 million people living in tents. The animals owned by the Israelites were drinking up the water and eating up the grass. This provoked Balak, the king of Moab, to initiate a "spiritual" remedy to destroy these unwanted visitors.

There was a noted seer living in Moab, a prophet named Balaam. His notoriety was his gift to speak prophetically and what he predicted always came to pass. He was hired by Moab's king to stand on a mountain overlooking Israel's encampment and speak curses over the Israelites. The king wanted disfavor to fall upon Israel. He wanted something bad to happen that would "overcome them and drive them out" (Num. 22:11). Despite God's warning not to go, the rebellious prophet (Balaam) rode his donkey to the edge of the mountain overlook. The Almighty spoke to him, warning him not to curse Israel:

> *"And God said unto Balaam, Thou shalt not go with them; thou shalt not curse the people: for they are blessed."*
>
> – Numbers 22:12

When Balaam opened his mouth, only words of blessing flowed out. The king rebuked him, moving him to a different location, hoping a different view would change his prophetic outlook. Again, prophetic blessings poured out as fast as Balaam could speak. Balaam disappointed the king when he said:

> *"How shall I curse, whom God hath not cursed? or how shall I defy, whom the Lord hath not defied?"*
>
> – Numbers 23:8

Balaam blessed Israel three times (Num. 24:10). It was clear that Balaam could not and would not abuse his prophetic gift to curse something that God had blessed. However, a strange twist suddenly stepped to the stage. A new type of strategy was plotted that would mark Balaam's name to be forever tagged as a compromising prophet placed in God's hall of shame.

THE STRANGE NEW STRATEGY

Balaam knew that he could not speak a curse against Israel. However, he understood that the Israelite God was very strict in His moral laws concerning His people. Balaam knew that the only way for Israel to lose God's blessing would be if the men or women would commit a horrid sin, provoking God's anger toward them, lifting His favor from them. A plot was conspired to slowly move the hearts of Israel into Baal worship. The game-plan included sending as many beautiful Moabite women into Israel's camp to mingle with the young men, seducing them into committing fornication. If the men yielded to this temptation, God would be required to judge then punish all involved.

The conspiracy was set in motion. Moabite women were sent to mingle throughout the camp, stirring up the passions of morally weak Hebrew men, tempting them to yield to sexual temptation. God saw it all, knowing if this sin of fornication went unchecked, the desire to sin would spread faster than cancer, infecting the entire nation. A plague of judgment struck. The idolatry and sexual sins led to the deaths of twenty-four thousand people (Num. 25:9).

Notice Balaam's involvement in this plot:

> *"Look, these women caused the children of Israel, through the counsel of Balaam, to trespass against the Lord in the incident of Peor, and there was a plague among the congregation of the Lord."*
>
> – Numbers 31:16 (NKJV)

Balaam is again alluded to in a negative light in the book of Revelation.

> *"But I have a few things against thee, because thou hast there them that hold the doctrine of Balaam, who taught Balak to cast a stumbling block before the children of Israel, to eat things sacrificed unto idols, and to commit fornication."*
>
> – Revelation 2:14

Balaam's plot became a huge "stumbling block" to Israel. In Greek, the phrase *stumbling block* is *skandelon* and refers to the *bait on a trap that attracts an animal to it*. The Israelites were "baited" by seductive, beautiful women of Moab to sin against God. The bait included sacrifices to their idols and the thoughts of sexual pleasure. In the

Commandments Moses would receive, idolatry and adultery were both forbidden. Also, in the law, there was a series of blessings for obedience and curses for disobedience (Duet. 28).

THE SELF-CURSE

Before explaining how the Balaam strategy is working against America, permit me to explain the two types of "curses." There are curses spoken over you by *others* and the ones you speak over *yourself.* The best example of a self-curse occurs in the Apostle Peter's life. The self-curse is concealed in a Greek word study, recorded in the four gospels. Matthew 26:69-75 (NKJV) explains the event:

> *"Now Peter sat outside in the courtyard. And a servant girl came to him, saying, "You also were with Jesus of Galilee." But he denied it before them all, saying, "I do not know what you are saying." And when he had gone out to the gateway, another girl saw him and said to those who were there, "This fellow also was with Jesus of Nazareth." But again he denied with an oath, "I do not know the Man!" And a little later those who stood by came up and said to Peter, "Surely you also are one of them, for your speech betrays you." Then he began to curse and swear, saying, "I do not know the Man!" Immediately a rooster crowed. And Peter remembered the word of Jesus who had said to him, "Before the rooster crows, you will deny Me three times." So he went out and wept bitterly."*

Peter vowed to Christ that he would remain faithful, even joining Him in death. To confirm his loyalty, Peter carried a sword. Christ predicted Peter would deny Him when the rooster crowed the third time. While sitting by a fire, Peter was suddenly exposed as one of Christ's disciples. Reacting in fear, he blurted out and denied that he knew

Christ. The Greek word *denied* means *to reject, disavow, to contradict.* Each gospel records Peter's denial.

In Matthew 26:72-74, he denied with an *"oath"* and began to "curse and swear, 'I do not know him.'" Mark chapter 14:68-71 reports that Peter began to *"curse and swear, 'I do not know him.'"* In Luke 22:55-61, we read of various details revealing the time frame, but Luke omits the incident of swearing. The fourth writer, John, was present at Christ's trial. Several Jews and Romans knew John was a disciple, yet John was not afraid to be seen at the trial (John 18:25-27). Peter was fearful as he had just assaulted a known person with his sword. We read:

> *"And Simon Peter stood and warmed himself. They said therefore unto him, Art not thou also one of his disciples? He denied it, and said, I am not. One of the servants of the high priest, being his kinsman, whose ear Peter cut off, said, Did not I see thee in the garden with him? Peter then denied again: and immediately the cock crew."*

PETER CURSED HIMSELF

The most interesting part of Peter's journey of denial is concealed in a Greek word study. The writers mention three words: oath, swore, and cursed. In the states, we think that swearing or cursing is the use of profanity. However, when Peter cursed, the root form of the word is the same Greek word used in Galatians 1:9 and is translated as "accursed."

> *"As we have said before, so now I say again, if anyone preaches any other gospel to you than what you have received, let him be accursed."*
>
> – Galatians 1:9 (NKJV)

When Peter *cursed*, the Greek word used is "anathema," which means *"to declare one liable to the severest penalties"* (Mark 14:71). In

Greek, it means "something dedicated, especially dedicated to evil." As used in the New Testament era, it refers to a person who is cursed by ecclesiastical authority. It can be an announcement intended to banish or to excommunicate a person in the synagogue. According to Greek scholar Kenneth Wuest, what most Christians may not understand is when Peter said, "If I know the man, let me be accursed," he actually said, "Let me be anathema!" Wuest comments:

> *"But he began to be putting himself under a curse, and to be putting himself under oath, I do not know this man concerning whom you are speaking."*

"The word *anathema* has turned up in some ancient Greek sources and in Greek secular writings. In Greek writings, when something that was anathema was subject to destruction by the gods. Paul's use of the word anathema in Galatians 1:8, 9, "dedicated to god" in this context means under His curse."[1]

Peter was not on, what some would call, a "cussing streak." He was actually placing a *self-curse* upon himself. Jesus had warned Peter, "Satan has desired you that he may sift you as wheat; but I have prayed that your faith would not fail" (Luke 22:31). The word *fail* actually meant that his faith would not die. Jesus knew that Peter would place an "anathema" upon himself. In Jewish thought, Peter was saying that if he knew Christ, then let him be banished from the synagogue and the house of Israel. The Jews understood this as a method of discipline for anyone whose conduct was operating against the rules of God or the synagogue.[2] An anathema was a serious charge. Paul used this word when he wrote, "If any man loved not the Lord Jesus Christ, let him be Anathema" (1 Cor. 16:22). Something called anathema was doomed for destruction.

In Jewish thought, only the head rabbi in the synagogue could release someone from an anathema. In Peter's case, his "rabbi" (teacher and instructor) was Christ. After the resurrection, when Jesus confronted Peter, He asked him three times, "do you love me more than these?" Christ was erasing the shame and the sin of Peter denying Him three times, thus lifting this self-curse from Peter (John 21), demonstrating to him that his failure was forgiven. The Chief Rabbi and High Priest of heaven was welcoming Peter back into the fellowship of the disciples and into the church Christ was preparing.

HOW AMERICA IS WALKING UNDER A SELF-CURSE

America's founders were predominantly Bible reading and Bible-believing men of faith, *most* being professing Christians, honoring biblical principles. The Mayflower Compact and our founding documents (the Holy Scriptures and the rules from heaven), became our foundation for moral, judicial, and legislative laws and dogma. Just as the Almighty liberated the Hebrews from the tyranny of Pharaoh, these new "Israelites" were breaking ties with the Pharaoh of Britain and England.

America has been blessed because America's cornerstone of Democracy was constructed upon biblical principles, honoring God, and trusting Him as the source of our many blessings. However, changes began occurring in the early 1960s with the rise of rationalism, humanism, atheism, liberalism, and progressivism. These combined dogmas and philosophies planted four to five decades of tares (poisonous weeds and thorns), choking out our spiritual heritage, leading to the elimination or altering of moral absolutes, rejecting any biblical rules.

How can the kingdom of darkness plot a curse upon America that would provoke God? The strategy is rooted in Balaam. The kingdom of darkness plans to energize the enactment of the same plot that initiated judgment on the Hebrews over 3,500 years ago. America's new laws and social injustices are provoking the covenant of our ancestors (Lev. 26:45). Signing forbidden acts into law can open the door for an eventual national self-curse. When the Supreme Court legalized abortion in 1973, and in 2010, when they legalized same-sex marriage, the nation legally permitted what the scriptures rejected.

The only spiritual thread our nation is still hanging by is the prayers and intercession of a faithful remnant scattered throughout the fifty states. Righteousness is a restraining force. When Lot was living in Sodom, the angels revealed that God would not send destruction to the city until Lot, his wife, and two daughters were out of the Sodom:

> *"And he said to him, "See, I have favored you concerning this thing also, in that I will not overthrow this city for which you have spoken. Hurry, escape there. For I cannot do anything until you arrive there."*
>
> – GENESIS 19:21-22 (NJKV)

Abraham was promised the entire land of Canaan. He and God sealed the agreement with Abraham in an early blood covenant. In reality, the five cites in the valley south of the Dead Sea — four doomed to destruction — were a part of Abraham's covenant-inheritance as they were built on Abraham's God-given land grant. God would not destroy the cities until He first met with Abraham. Both he and God came to an agreement. If a small remnant of ten righteous persons could be found in Sodom, then Sodom and the other cities would escape God's wrath, and mercy would be extended (Gen. 18).

REVERSING THE SELF-CURSE

We must never forget, *whatever sin brings on, repentance can bring off.* The word repent is used throughout the New Testament and means to reconsider your spiritual or moral lifestyle, see your sin or errors, regret your actions, and begin thinking differently. Godly sorrow (2 Cor. 7:10) includes a sense of remorse for your actions. Often, when a believer commits a sin or trespass, the Holy Spirit pierces their conscience with *conviction*, arresting a person, stopping them in their path. Many times, a believer responds to God's convicting power by telling the Lord they are sorry for their actions. However, if a person does not change their thinking or carnal ways, they will live in a repetitive cycle of telling God, "I am sorry," without changing their actions. True repentance is a sense of regret, a sincere prayer of asking for forgiveness, and a change (transformation) within your heart and mind. Paul wrote to be "...transformed by the renewing of your mind" (Rom. 12:2).

Once a person has repented, entering into a redemption covenant with Christ through His blood, they are released from the curses of the law. Paul taught that "Christ has redeemed us from the curses of the Law being made a curse for us" (Gal. 3:13). Just as individual curses are removed by true repentance and forsaking your wicked ways, national curses are removed when repentance comes, resulting from governmental and spiritual leaders joining in a call of repentance and prayer with the people uniting in obedience. The Assyrian city of Nineveh was marked for destruction. During a forty-day "grace period," the king demanded the entire city fast and pray, putting on sackcloth and sitting in ashes. God forgave their nation's sins, giving them a reprieve that continued for over 150 years.

The 9-11 Al-Qaeda terror attacks struck New York City, paralyzing the entire world in shock, followed by rage and anger. The horrific assaults provided a brief opportunity for those leading the nation from New York City and Washington, D.C., not just to join in prayer and sing "God bless America" but to repent. In ancient Israel, the prophets would have called for humility before God in national repentance and fasting. For half of America and for most politicians, a call for repentance is too radical. Americans instead focused on renewing a spirit of flag-waving patriotism, uniting around a just cause, destroying those who had plotted to destroy America's economic center. This makes me feel great and proud of the nation, but eventually, we forget and turn back to our wicked ways.

The real secret to America's foundation of prosperity and success is found in the lives of faithful and spiritual men and women who believed they must live and follow a "Higher-Law." In Babylon, new Persian and Babylonian laws were enforced, contradicting the Divine Higher-Laws. Daniel and his companions made it clear to angry Babylonian authorities that whether they lived or died in a burning furnace or a den of lions, they would never submit to any law of man that forbid them from praying or diminished their religious freedom. It is time we grow some *Babylonian backbone* so that we stand taller than the burning verbal slander sent to scorch our faith.

I have taught my children and ministry friends that we must live by the principles and instruction revealed in the Scripture, love God, and love one another. Jesus proved it possible to build a tough shield to resist the enemy's darts while keeping a tender heart to love others. Just as Christ, we must maintain wax-free ears to hear the still small voice of the heavenly Father. Above all, we must avoid the Balaam strategy.

CHAPTER 7

NECESSARY RESISTANCE:
ELIJAH AND JEZEBEL—THE COMING CLASH

Bookstores are filled with hundreds of books documenting historic rebellions and revolutions. America has been, and presently is, a politically, socially, and morally divided nation, sadly similar to the level of division prior to the American Civil War. On almost any public poll conducted, with spiritual, moral, or social questions, the percentages usually stand at 50% for and 50% against. One half represents a conservative, pro-Constitution, flag-waving, Bible-reading army versus social progressives, mingled with some violent extremists, forcing a hateful, radical agenda on others that appeals to the left. It is clear, the lava is heating up, and the volcano is preparing to erupt. The crack of the fault line is under pressure and will soon rip, and the F-5 storm is building energy as it prepares to spin the destruction of free speech from coast to coast. The Apostle Paul penned a preview of this moment.

THE ROOTS OF A REBELLION

In 2 Thessalonians 2, Paul presented a prophetic forecast to look for prior to the revealing of the "man of sin, the son of perdition" (meaning destruction), who is the biblical Antichrist. Before his arrival, a major sign will be "the falling away," which, according to Paul, must occur first (2 Thess. 2:3). The phrase "falling away" in Greek is the word *apostasy,* which refers to "a defection, a revolt, a rebellion, to stand away from the truth."[1] Since this verse was written to the church, this defection would be a defection against truth in general, especially spiritual truth. In particular, individuals turning away from the laws of God. In this chapter, Paul also notes a rise in lawlessness.

There are three types of uprisings fomented when actions or information is rejected, seeding rebellions against authority, including a resistance to the particular controversy. The first is a *religious-centered resistance.* The Protestant Reformation Movement, commenced by Martin Luther in 1517, was a religious movement that splintered the theological, political, and cultural ideas in Western Europe, which was, at the time, predominantly Catholic. This split in theology and ideology gave an opportunity for a new Christian group to splinter from the old system. This new religious movement called Protestantism spread throughout Western Europe and created an unpassable rift with the Pope and the Catholic church. For many years, fighting persisted between Protestant followers and the traditional Catholics. The Protestant resisters experienced verbal and physical persecution from the Roman Church, especially targeting any and all Protestant reform leaders.

The second split is a *moral division* between religious beliefs based upon the moral absolutes of the Bible, clashing with anti-biblical theories based upon a mix of secularism and humanism. One divisive issue is abortion. To the biblically literate, abortion is the act is taking the life of a living, breathing human. On the opposing side, abortion is a medical procedure to terminate an unwanted pregnancy. Those against it are labeled "Pro-Life," and those in favor are marked as "Pro-Choice." Both sides believe they have the truth on the subject, and each side protests the beliefs of the opposing side.

The third type of rebellion is a *political uprising* based upon unsustainable national debt and creepy social ideas such as allowing a man to freely use a woman's restroom or change in a woman's dressing room area. Social resistance often begins with pockets of protesters slowly gaining attention and followers. The small minority soon turns into a huge multitude, exploding into a national revolution, climaxing with the forcible overthrow of a government or social order in favor of a new system. Two political revolutions come to mind. The first is the 1917 Bolshevik Revolution directed by leftist revolutionary Vladimir Lenin, who opened the door to the rise of Communism in Russia. The second is the ascent of Fascism directed by the Third Reich in Germany that boosted the popularity of Adolph Hitler, eventually bringing this dictator of death to his evil throne.

Political revolutions occur when the general population believes that their governmental leadership is *corrupt or oppressive* or when the nation is on its way to being bankrupt through economic turmoil, heading into a downward death-spiral and massive job layoffs. If taxpaying citizens observe a massive rise in taxes, uncontrolled spending, fiscal abuse, or political incompetence, including outright corruption, these perceptions become the tip of the spear for an aggressive revolt. The frustration of the common worker becomes the broom to sweep out "corrupt" politicians or completely change the entire social order with a new order. These are the types of revolutions that often turn violent.

AMERICA — RIPE FOR ANOTHER REVOLUTION

Americans have observed those on the left create their protest movements, successfully organizing their uprisings, which too often turns violent. It seems (from the left) that the protests gain national or international attention, hoping to turn public opinion toward favoring their agenda. Among the radical left, their perception is that peaceful protests get very little attention that brings change. However, by turning aggressive or destructive, their grievances are the highlight of all cable news, attracting larger audiences. When leftist-extremists are burning businesses, cars, and yards, they seem to get gentle hand slaps from their socialist co-conspirators in Washington, who spin the violence, excusing the staged outrage, unless of course, similar violence comes to their own back doors from the opposing side. According to the ancient Greek philosopher Aristotle, there are two types of revolutions, one which brings a complete change from one constitution to another, and the other brings a modification of an existing constitution.[2] The new Socialist-Democrats clearly hope to rewrite the U.S. Constitution tilting the state and national political scales in their direction. Their discussions for "change" include adding two new states (D.C. and Puerto Rico), loading the Supreme Court with liberal-Socialist judges, and opening the border, allowing hundreds of thousands to enter the nation, a guaranteed voting group for generations to come.

When President Trump was elected in 2016, the Democratic party leaders in the House and Senate spent four years making every attempt to demonize, criticize, and ostracize him, including using false or embellished information, along with organizing secret spying rings against him, hoping to bring down his presidency, including impeaching him—twice. Discerning conservative Americans saw just how far unscrupulous politicians and government agencies will go to carry out an inside political assassination. They discovered that lies are permitted if the false scenario favors the opposing side. Their Russian Collusion allegations had so little "truth" they eventually fell apart like a paper mâché southern-border wall.

After the 2020 election, there was mounting evidence that there were huge vote discrepancies, including thousands of dead voters, votes counted twice, more votes than there were registered voters, underage voters, and machines that had shifted votes. After two months, it was evident that state legislators, governors, courts, including the Supreme Court, the House, and Senate, and most of the media, with the exception of a few, refused to expose or even discuss possible fraud. Most states rejected the call for internal audits. To tens of millions of Americans, this created a perception that this was a pre-planned event directed by the so-called Deep State Cabal who was in on the scam, corrupting the voting system in America. True or not, the lack of investigation made millions believe the system could never again be trusted.

The dam holding back the waters of alleged "conspiracy theories" blew apart when major social media giants chose to ban Trump and those in his inner circle, including lawyers, when they threatened to go direct to the people by posting video interviews on all social media platforms. It soon became evident to patriots and conservatives that anyone who supported the president or believed the election was "rigged" was painted as an ignorant right-winged extremist and should be silenced in every manner possible.

The perception of corruption, manipulation, and deception from the "swamp" has been building for many years, energizing a different type of *American Revolution*. Tables began turning when frustrated Americans started confronting politicians in Washington airports, screaming at them, calling them "traitors." On one flight, some people were chanting "traitor" at a Utah politician sitting in business class. One woman stopped on the street in New York and interrupted Chuck Schumer, a Democratic Senator from New York, who was Trump's thorn in the flesh, harassing him for four years. She verbally raked Schumer over the coals. Good, hard-working, God-fearing Americans sat back with the fire of a furnace boiling in their spirit. Suddenly, the restraint began cracking, and the heat was unleashed. America's momma and daddy bears were and are now awake. The wide divide between conservatives and liberals is looking more like the Grand Canyon than a small political rift.

THE DIVIDED STATES OF AMERICA

America's political and historical pattern runs parallel with ancient Israel. Originally, the land of Israel was divided into twelve plots of land among the twelve sons of Jacob. Although there were twelve distinct tribes, with tens of thousands of men in each tribe, these twelve were united as one in their spiritual, moral, and cultural beliefs. This unity in the kingdom of Israel continued for 480 years, beginning from the time Israel returned from Egypt through the forty years of King Solomon's rule.

After Solomon's death, his unwise son (Rehoboam) ascended the throne, becoming solely responsible for a massive split of his grandfather David's monarchy. The twelve tribes split into *northern* and *southern* kingdoms. Ten tribes broke off, joining a ten-tribe coalition in the north. They selected a new king and a new priest who would lighten the financial burden that Solomon had left them from paying for his massive building programs in Jerusalem, Megiddo, and other locations. The older generation was tired of carrying the financial taxation-burden of the nation, while the younger generation had not sacrificed at all. They ignored the advice of Israel's elders, recklessly advising Rehoboam to demean the old people, warning them that he would add more burdens to them, "chastising them with scorpions" (1 Kings 12:8-14). The ten tribes rebelled, choosing Jeroboam as their king. Judah and Benjamin, two tribes in the south, remained loyal, staying connected with Jerusalem since Rehoboam was David's descendant. The division was not caused by some spiritual division but from *economic* hardships.

Another impact of this split was the refusal of the northern tribes to join the southern tribes for the seven yearly festivals to worship at the Temple in Jerusalem. This action led to the ten tribes eventually backsliding into idolatry and perversion. The land allocations of two southern tribes, Judah and Benjamin, bordered the Temple in Jerusalem, the headquarters for the true prophets and priests who lived and worked there. This north-south division is eerily similar. In America, there is a clear division between the spiritual and moral beliefs of Americans living in the northeast and those living in the southern states. One northern House member in Washington, D.C., made the statement that the left could pass their agenda, but the people in the south were hindering it. There is a visible barrier between America's northeast and west coast liberal-thinkers and the conservatives living in the southern and mid-western states. In the northeast, the primary religion, past and present, is Catholicism, while the south leans more Protestant. Both religious groups are targeted with repression for their pro-life ideas and supporting traditional marriage. There is also a division concerning the rising national debt and unbridled government spending. Progressives wish to raise taxes, paying for government subsidies as the opposing side demands to cut government spending, including the so-called "pork" in spending bills. The conservative-south holds firm to the Constitution while the northeastern and west coast Senators and Congresspersons often attempt to execute laws that would completely change our founding father's rules and ideas. Basically, the progressives want more government, and the conservatives want to be left alone with little to no government control or restrictions.

THE EVER-PRESENT SPIRITUAL CLASH

There have been and will be spiritual clashes in America that I call "The spirit of Elijah battling the spirit of Jezebel." In the days of Elijah, a national confrontation existed between the righteous and the unrighteous created by a religiously repressive governmental administration in Samaria under the tight-fists of King Ahab and his utterly wicked wife, Jezebel. This criminal queen set her agenda on silencing all prophetic voices, as true prophets were exposing her and her husband as sinful, wicked puppets of evil that were destined for God's tribunal. With fiery indignation, she commissioned a personal delegation of "head-hunters" to decapitate every true prophet of Israel that crossed their path. The threat of premature death terrified thousands of prophets, sending them into exile to live in rugged, dark caves scattered throughout Israel. Jezebel's goal was to silence all men (prophets) who opposed her in any manner.

The "spirit of Elijah" (meaning similar *characteristics* of Elijah) and the spirit of Jezebel (meaning the *characteristics* of Jezebel) reappear in the New Testament. Before his conception, the angel Gabriel predicted that John the Baptist would come "in the spirit and power of Elijah" (Luke 1:17). John never performed one miracle, yet he preached with such wisdom, power, and boldness, living in the wilderness similar to Elijah. In another narrative, King Herod, the regional Gentile leader, was lusting after a young woman seductively dancing before him. In a moment of passion, he promised her whatever she desired. Her mother manipulated the moment, insisting the head of John the Baptist be delivered on a silver platter. Herod succumbed to her pressure, beheading John (Matt. 14:1-11). This is the *spirit* of Jezebel. This woman detested John's preaching, as John was publicly rebuking Herod for his immoral lifestyle. The angel Gabriel said John would minister in the "spirit (boldness) of Elijah." Jezebel went after Elijah's head (1 Kings 19:2), and this evil woman went after the head of John the Baptist. Elijah survived, but John did not. Both women put a bullseye on the head of a prophet.

Another *Jezebel* reappears in the New Testament where a female *calling herself* a prophetess was controlling (or sexually seducing) men in the church. She was also corrupting the people with false doctrines. God gave her a season or a "space to repent." If she refused to repent, God promised to, as we would say, *lay the hammer down*, giving this false prophetess a permanent chastisement that would conclude with her death (Rev. 2:20-23).

Escaping Jezebel's deathtrap, the prophet Elijah was transported alive to heaven in a chariot of fire (2 Kings 2). Malachi 4:5 predicts that God will send the prophet Elijah to earth "before the great and dreadful day of the Lord to turn the hearts of children to the fathers." The fulfillment of this verse is detailed in Revelation 11, where the Apostle John observed two men, both were prophets, ministering in Israel during the first forty-two months of the Tribulation. One of these men is Elijah, and he will reappear at the end of days. Since Elijah reappears at the end of days, then it stands to reason that the spirit of Jezebel, *the spirit seeking to silence the truth*, cut off the authority of prophetic voices, or send them into the caves of silence, will rise again in *political* power. In the United States, this same spirit is now pulling the strings of its puppets in high places.

If Jezebel, the queen of control, were living today and were in political or business leadership, she would be elected Speaker of the House in the U.S. House of Representatives, become the CEO over the New York Times, serve on the board of all cable News Networks, and would be overseeing the Social Media companies from her glass skyscraper in Silicon Valley, ensuring that only the voices stroking her ego, or agreeing with her idolatrous agenda would be approved for national distribution. How can this generation, the remnant of truth-seekers and God-fearers, challenge and overcome the Jezebel spirit?

THE KEY IS JOHN THE BAPTIST

God's kingdom will not be overwhelmed, neither His kingdom overcome! We will not fall to the gates of hell or bow to an army of Jezebels. The preview of what God has planned for the true church is found in the pattern of John the Baptist. John was assigned as a forerunner to prepare the way for Christ (John 1:23). John represents the final end-time generation God will raise up prior to the return of the Lord, including a generation of youth who will serve God, preparing the way for the return of the King.

The parallels of John's birth are key patterns pointing to an end-time generation of youth, destined to spearhead the world-wide Joel 2 revival. First, John was born from a barren womb. His mother was old and had never given birth. However, through continuous prayers of both her and her husband, who served as an older priest at the temple, the aged couple was blessed with a son. Malachi wrote that the spirit of Elijah assists in bringing the children and the spiritual fathers together (Mal. 4:5). The final outpouring of the Spirit, predicted in Joel 2:28-29, involves both youth and adults. John was young, and his parents were old. The Holy Spirit released prophetic words through both parents, Elizabeth and Zacharias (Luke 1 and 2). Second, John was filled with the Spirit from his mother's womb, which was unheard of until this moment in history (Luke 1:15). This agrees with Joel's prediction that "sons and daughters" would receive the Holy Spirit. John was an infant, growing within his mother's womb, yet the Lord filled him with the Holy Spirit. We think of adults, older mature Christians, as candidates for the Spirit's baptism (Matt. 3:11). However, in this pattern and prophecy, the children, the "babes" in Christ, meaning the immature youth, will experience a true spiritual encounter.

John was in Elizabeth's womb six months when she met her cousin Mary, who told of her encounter with Gabriel, announcing she would conceive of the Holy Ghost, a son, who would be the Messiah. Elizabeth said, "As soon as your voice sounded in my ears, the babe (John) leaped in my womb for joy" (Luke 1:44). This verse prophetically indicates that the youth, in this final revival, will "leap" or be vibrant and demonstrative in their worship. Their worship will be an overflow of the joy they are experiencing! You see this very type of worship in the majority of all Christian youth conferences in America and abroad.

I was honored to minister to thousands of young people at a gathering called "The Ramp." Toward the conclusion of the message, I sensed a very strong presence of the Lord overshadow me. I heard the still small voice of the Holy Spirit saying, "This is the generation that can save the nation." Men may control politics. However, God controls the prophecies. Biblical history shows us how to get out from under the control and manipulation of the Jezebel spirit. It is by praying down the rain (Holy Spirit) and the fire (the zeal of the Lord) by the anointing of the Holy Spirit.

THE SONS OF THE PROPHETS

Few people are aware that Elijah organized schools for the prophets located in Bethel and Jericho. These were the sons born to the prophets in Israel. In Elijah's day, the true prophets were in exile, silenced in fear. When Elijah was to be taken to heaven, he stopped by both schools to visit and speak a final word with these younger men. The scripture identifies fifty strong men from the Jericho school that organized a three-day search party looking for Elijah's body (2 Kings 2:16). Although the old and seasoned prophet Elijah was going to be with the Lord in a chariot of fire, he left the student he mentored, Elisha, in charge of the schools of the prophets. Elijah knew that Jezebel was still in the land, and this younger generation must be taught to pray, prophesy, and defeat Jezebel and any seed from her that would arise in the future. Perhaps this is why in the last days, sons and daughters will prophesy. They will become like John the Baptist and will not allow their authority to be cut off, and they will refuse to be silent to sin and injustice.

Remember, if a spirit of Jezebel arises, so will the spirit of Elijah. The political and spiritual clash is coming. We must raise up more Elijah's in this closing generation.

CHAPTER 8

GOING UNDERGROUND: THE SECRET STRATEGIES OF OPPRESSED PEOPLE

Those who believe in religious and personal freedoms need an "Insiders Rule Book." Our present issue is how can Christians and true patriotic Americans tap into a non-violent approach in defending the totality of our freedoms, helping prevent America's 50 states and their individual citizens from being chained to a corrupt, selfish, egotistical leader and their legislation when some believe their assignment is to remove outdated religious beliefs from America's new progressive culture? We have seen the shady political machine use the tactic of freezing financial accounts, stopping church loans, or in one national case, emptying business accounts from a business, fining them over $130,000 for not closing under state COVID laws. What can be done to protest and stop such utter nefarious activity?

TWO FOUNDATIONAL SCRIPTURES

I will present this *insider information* using two noted comments made by Christ as a foundation. The first is a parable involving a wealthy landowner that hired one man to oversee his estate. The man, called a steward, had underperformed, failing to collect large debts from two debtors. Under a threat of being fired, the steward met with the two businessmen, both owing his boss large sums. Instead of demanding the full payment, he reduced their debts, collected the money, erasing the rest of the debts owed, also providing his boss some needed cash. The boss commended him on such a unique strategy. As *a little of something is better than nothing at all.* Christ concluded this parable with this statement, "For the children of this world are in their generation wiser than the children of light" (Luke 16:1-8).

Christ's second statement is how we must use wisdom when operating in the world's system. Christ said, "Behold I send you forth as sheep in the midst of wolves: be ye therefore wise as serpents and harmless as doves" (Matt. 10:16). A serpent conceals itself from its enemies. It hides until it senses danger, then strikes. Some serpents blend in with their natural surroundings, making them difficult to detect until you are suddenly standing near them. A dove is a gentle bird that does not retaliate when attacked. When Jesus was physically threatened, He took His disciples and fled to a secret place away from people. He never physically retaliated against His enemies but used wise words and spiritual authority to expose their hypocrisy while instructing and ministering to multitudes of common people who were being oppressed by the Roman occupation.

As Christians who know Scripture and are in covenant with God, we are against all forms of violence. Here is a thought to radical protesters. If you want to burn something, burn your *own* house, your *own* car, and your *own* business and stop destroying other people's property. Would you be so lame as to break into your own mother's home, overturning furniture, breaking the dishes, then walk out dragging the flat-screen television along with her personal computer? Yet, these face-covered wild donkeys have willfully destroyed and stolen from other people in numerous cities. Violence only breeds violence. God warned, saying, "Whoever sheds man's blood, by man shall his blood be shed…" (Gen. 9:6).

Our goal to rescue America from the brink must be done without guns, breaking glass, or burning property. Our methods must be wise as a serpent without physically harming others. If we wish to vote in the right leaders, then we need to learn a few lessons from the left. The reason Georgia elected two socialist Senators was because between the Presidential election and the state Senate runoff, the Democrats organized and registered 75,000 new voters. One woman in Georgia, who lost an election, organized a movement that allegedly registered 800,000 new voters for the 2020 election. While the Republicans were just hoping everyone would show up, the opposing side was putting action to their strategy. Elections are won by the *go-vote* and not the *hope-vote.* Is it any wonder that this normally Republican state went Democrat in the Senatorial election?

WHAT CHRISTIANS IN COMMUNIST NATIONS TAUGHT ME

On November 19, 1989, when the Berlin Wall was hammered and chiseled into rubbles of concrete, uniting eastern and western Germany, other Eastern Block Communist nations had already begun their journey of independence from the Soviet Union. I was invited to two Communist nations, Romania and Bulgaria, within a year after they were opened for western ministers to preach in churches. Floyd Lawhon, Jentezen Franklin, and I, preached some of the first gospel meetings in large halls and auditoriums in both countries shortly after the changes in the government.

In Romania, many ministers were still fearful of possible retaliation. As people began worshipping loud, I remember the older men in the church closing all the doors and windows, checking down the street for the secret police. Keeping worship quiet was still in their nature after forty years of repression. In one Romanian city, after booking a large hall, all of the posters inviting the people to attend had been torn down by men who were still linked with the Communists. When returning to the hotel, my interpreter noted a plain-clothed secret police member standing outside of our hotel room.

In Bulgaria, in a city near the Turkish border, an auditorium was booked for a small team and me to minister. Our flights were delayed by fog in Switzerland, causing us to miss the first few days. We later learned that the first night we were to minister, a terrorist bombed the facility, blowing glass onto the sidewalks. Had we been there, we could have been injured. In both nations, the Orthodox priests would resist these "Protestant meetings," especially when their own members began attending the services to hear the Bible lessons taught.

I asked the leaders how they functioned under Communism, and the answer was, "By going 'underground' and by only communicating with trusted contacts."

The first lesson I discovered in both nations was their "secret weapon," which was prayer and learning to hear the still small voice of the Holy Spirit. Because their phones were always "bugged," any plans for a secret prayer gathering or a small meeting for teaching could not be announced in public or on a phone call. The believers would literally pray and know where a meeting was being held without ever being told. This spiritual sensitivity to hear the Lord's voice is lacking in America as we have never had to operate on this level, and too many churches believe "God does not speak today." With where this country is going, these unbelieving believers better reconsider their belief that God has put a muzzle over His mouth.

There were three major points the ministers in these nations gave me that may one day be important for any freedom-loving American. First, instead of using any communication that was trackable, they used hand-written notes, passing out the information, then sharing it face-to-face in certain locations to avoid suspicion from the Communist authorities. The notes were later burned. Second, when having a prayer meeting or a Bible study, the numbers remained small, usually under 10 people to avoid suspicion from the Communist police and secret spies, who dressed in everyday clothes, as most unregistered religious gatherings were illegal. The third aspect was vetting anyone who may be posing as a new Christian trying to get on the inside to collect information on behalf of local authorities. If a Christian was suspicious, that person was never allowed into any inner-circle or ever privy to secret information as they could be "planted" or a "spy." Paul alluded to these types of *spiritual spies* when he warned the church:

> *"And that because of false brethren unawares brought in, who came in privily to spy out our liberty which we have in Christ Jesus, that they might bring us into bondage."*
>
> – Galatians 2:4

It was always the inner voice of the Holy Spirit that revealed the true believers from the false ones. At times, the Communist leaders in local cities would attempt to cut off phone services, ration fuel supplies, or cut off electricity to Christian's homes or meetings they were having. Ministers and church leaders often kept additional fuel in safe places and had contacts using other forms of communication if needed. One of the main bishops of the Church of God in Bulgaria had been under house arrest numerous times and beaten on several occasions to intimidate him. He was often followed. He assigned other individuals to travel and do ministry work. As the old expression implies, while the

Communist police had their focus on his left hand, he was continuing to minister to the underground church with his right hand.

BLOCK HOW COMPANIES HEAR AND SEE YOU

I learned the following from a former security expert and from missionaries that travel undercover in Communist nations, secretly providing Bibles. The security expert (whom I will not name) had been inside high-level U.S. agencies. He was visiting me and said, "Give me your cell phone." He placed his and my phone in a large porcelain jar and closed the lid. He told me that this would help prevent someone from hearing the conversation through the phones' speaker. I thought he might be a bit overactive until he explained to me what phone towers and certain information collection companies were able to do with a cell phone, including one just sitting around. The best way to block any signal from coming in or going out is to place electronic devices in a lead-lined bag. These bags were used to protect sensitive photography film from being erased by older airport x-ray machines. The fellow then asked about any laptop computers in the office. This was when he reminded me that a CEO of a major computer corporation places tape over the microphone and camera on his laptop. This was also done before we began speaking. When discussing information with members of the underground church, we always remove all phones from the room.

I mentioned this to a friend on one occasion when he held up his phone and said, "Watch this." He held his finger over the camera and speaker, and a message came up saying, "Please uncover your camera and microphone." We both just stared at each other.

When a missionary friend was outside of the United States, I was told that should I text, I was never to use their name or any information about where they were or their assignment. Once outside of the U.S., this person would send a text using dashes, breaking up keywords, as texts in many modern nations are fed through computers, looking for keywords, and if those words are found, the text can be viewed by a person monitoring messages. If we talked on the phone, there were certain words to never use, as they were "trigger words" picked up by specialized computer programs. This person traveled to very dangerous areas to minister.

Another method to block communication listening devices is to play loud music throughout the room. One group knew they were being listened to by special devices. Each time they needed to discuss a strategy, they would sit in a vehicle and run it several times through a car wash which interfered with the "spies" signal. Ministers in Communist nations would also communicate face-to-face or in writing, then when finished, shred the papers, or better yet, have them burned. These may seem like crude methods, but when Communism and Socialism have their special police ready to arrest ministers in meetings or to prevent them from spreading the gospel, these men had to learn how to "go around the system."

In 2020-2021, in America, individuals and corporations began writing on Facebook about exposing voter fraud. Suddenly, they found their pages flagged or banned. This is because certain phrases involving "voter fraud" were marked as "trigger words" and were read and flagged by fact-checkers. One way to write the phrase would be V-t-er-F-au-d. One high-level advisor told me in 2018 to address them in text or e-mail communications by speaking of the President as Mr. D or Don, or D.T. This is the same method leftist politicians in Washington use when sending e-mails or texts to avoid detailing a person's name.

In one Asian nation, when ministers come into the country, they come in as businessmen. If they are ministering, they ride motorcycles driven by secret believers but never ride the same one to a final destination. Every few miles, the system is set up to quickly stop, jump off one and on to another one, then a third and fourth, before arriving at their destination. This is planned far in advance, and the plan is known only to the drivers. This is to lose anyone that may be following them.

These are important methods of communicating for the oppressed and monitored multitudes living in Communist and radical Socialist nations. Under Communism, much of the buying and selling was done through the "black market," using the currency of each country. I am certainly not promoting this form of transaction for Americans. I do suggest having cash out in the event that individual bank accounts are frozen, which happened to some people we knew living in Georgia in early January 2021. Their "crime" was they had attended a Trump Rally in D.C.

Many European countries, including China, have thousands of cameras in major cities using facial recognition when people are walking the streets, shopping, or banking. I have no fear of this technology. If you are doing nothing wrong, there is not much to fear. However, it is interesting to note that during most conservative protests, people are showing their faces without masking them. All the while, during a radical left protest, most have masks covering their entire face. The difference is the conservatives have planned no violence, while the radical left has prepared, covering their faces to prevent being identified by facial recognition or exposed later on television.

BACK TO VOTING

Many good, patriotic Americans now believe their vote no longer matters. There are 234 million people who are eligible to vote in America. However, not all of those are registered to vote. According to USA Today, there were 159 million ballots cast in the 2020 presidential election. This accounts for 66.7 percent of the eligible voters.

Let us use the 70 million who voted for Trump. There were tens of thousands who did not vote at all. The first step to changing leadership at a state or national level is to have all registered voters actually *show up and vote.* The math is simple. Suppose each of the 70 million voters register one new voter or inspires one person who did not vote to vote conservative. In that case, the number of "new" votes becomes tens of millions, assuming they all vote for the same *candidate.*

The radical left is not afraid to protest. They wave signs, scream through bullhorns, throw rocks, bottles, and garbage, gaining free media attention, which is one reason for the protests. Protesters are organized nation-wide, using e-mails, texts, and Social Media. For conservatives, there are many times when a peaceful protest is necessary, demonstrating to state and national leaders that there is either support or rejection for a certain platform.

I have met and enjoyed meals with former congresspersons, governors, and mayors. In conversations, several informed me that personal, professionally written letters sent to their offices receive attention, especially when, in one day, the mail is filled with letters from their district or state. They know a person is serious if they take time to write and mail their feelings as this requires thought on the issues they are addressing. The letter should be written on a letterhead if possible, typed and printed on a quality printer, and look more like a business letter. Also, letters with numerous signatures are important. For letter length, one or two pages and getting to the point is the best.

There is also e-mail and other forms of communication. E-mails should be to the point and have your name. E-mails without names and addresses are at times ignored and put into "File 13," the junk pile marked for the shredder. If you are not serious enough to use your name and address, you will not be taken seriously. *Never make any threat to an elected public official, as this can be considered a serious crime.*

THE PULPIT CHALLENGE

In my opinion, one of America's biggest weaknesses has been the subject matter being released from behind the pulpits. Ministers of the Gospel who have a calling from God to minister are not "spiritual gurus," "life coaches," or "motivational speakers." We are to be teachers and preachers of God's Word and must not treat preaching as though we are walking through a cafeteria line, picking and choosing what will please someone else's taste.

Think about the subjects that our culture speaks about every day that we never hear dealt with in pulpits. When was the last time you heard a minister explain the following:

- Why we believe abortion is wrong?
- When does the eternal spirit enter the fetus?
- Why we believe life begins at conception?
- Why being a virgin is connected to a biblical blood covenant?
- Why God ordained marriage between a man and a woman?
- Why God hates racial injustices, and what should we do to resolve them?

An entire generation is neck-deep in the mire of ignorance because of ministers refusing to dive into the deep waters of some "controversial subject." Yet, there is a society that is wanting to know "why" we believe what we believe.

POLITICS IN THE PULPIT

The primary message to be preached behind the pulpit is the redemptive covenant through Christ that, when believed, brings a person eternal life (John 3:16). Messages must include salvation, faith, principles for Christian living, prophecy, spiritual warfare, the Holy Spirit, and teaching the doctrines of the Bible.

At the same time, the issues that we call "political hot potatoes," labeled as "political issues," are, in reality, spiritual issues. For example, shedding innocent blood such as abortion is a moral-spiritual issue. To defend God's covenant of marriage is not some political ideology. Marriage between a man and woman is the first covenant God established and must be defended using the laws and precepts of the Divine Scriptures.

Our generation has been brain-washed by misinformation that the Constitution teaches "separation of church and state." This is incorrect. The founders did not want America to be under the control of one church as the Church of England was the official church of the English, persecuting opposing beliefs. The progressives teach "separation of church and state" when, in reality, they desire the separation of God from America. Ministers have the right to teach issues related to what God's Word accepts and rejects and to do so without fear of reprisal from a Constitutional government.

LEARN TO STOP TALKING

The weakness most people have, including some Christians, patriots, and conservatives, is the tendency of wanting to always "speak your mind" or "tell you what they have heard," including repeating every rumor on their social media platform. These rumors, at times, lead to false or misinformation, later embarrassing those who continually blabbed out what they "knew" or thought they knew. Often, individuals are attempting to build an audience by marking their videos or writings as "Urgent!" "Breaking News!" "Must See!" There is certainly more discipline required when zipping your mouth than needed when moving your mouth.

Years ago, my Israeli tour guide, Gideon Shor, was talking about how Israeli military soldiers are taught the importance of keeping military secrets. He suddenly held up both hands and pointed upward with one finger on each hand. He asked, "How much is this?" I said, "two." He said, "No, it is eleven. For every person you tell a secret to, it is repeated, and eventually, eleven people will know." A man from New Mexico hid a treasure worth millions of dollars for treasure hunters to find. He was the only person to know the actual hiding place. They asked him, "Why didn't you tell at least one other person?" His reply was, "Two can keep a secret if one of them is dead."

The moral of this story is we may soon find ourselves in a situation where we are no longer able to speak freely. We may soon be banned or limited in our writings, video postings, and possibly our speech over television. We must discover who we can trust and who should be in our inner circle. When Christ went to trial, Herod attempted to provoke Him into saying things that would have actually gotten Him into trouble with the Jewish authorities. Jesus "never opened His mouth." There was a good reason for Him remaining silent. He knew He could call 12 legions (about 72,000) of angels to descend from heaven, deliver Him, and stop the entire redemptive plan of God. Thus, He was like a lamb going its own slaughter, "He opened not his mouth" (Isa 53).

Learn the wisdom of the persecuted Christians from around the world. There is a time to speak and a time to remain silent. The battle may need to be fought in secret and not in the open. In the end, we win. Between now and the end, the freedom battle has begun.

Finally, I recently asked a pastor from an underground movement what was the greatest key to surviving under persecution? He said, "Our greatest weapon is prayer but also praying in the Spirit." The Holy Spirit leads and guides you into all truth (John 16:13). By praying excessively in the Spirit or in the prayer language of the Spirit, the Lord can reveal secrets, including the secret plots of your enemies. The Spirit of the Lord releases warning dreams and visions, helping a person to escape possible danger, including dangerous people. We must learn to operate "off the grid," so-to-speak, and not wait until freedom is gone.

CHAPTER 9

THE WOMAN WHO WOULD BE PRESIDENT

In 2008 when Hillary Clinton ran for president, her biggest challenge was an Illinois Senator named Barak Obama. I thought this could be the moment the 1933 prediction would unfold. Obama outperformed her and won the election. However, she returned in 2016, with every media outlet projecting a huge victory over the "controversial" Donald J. Trump. Washington D.C. was prepared to accept her as the first woman president. The night of the election, before the vote was counted, Time Magazine already printed a magazine cover with Hilary's picture. The cover read, "Madame President." In a totally unexpected twist, Trump pulled off a shocking upset. I considered "Hillary's potential win" as the fulfillment of a prediction from a vision. It wasn't. Then came Biden and Harris. Before Biden's swearing-in ceremony, I was amazed to hear secular, progressive networks saying Harris would eventually be president as the state of Biden's health and mental capability was becoming more clear. Just what is this 1933-prediction?

The minister who went into a "trance," seeing a stunning seven-point vision, was a noted evangelist during a unique ministry season that Christian historians identify as "The Healing Revival." This amazing seven-year awakening began in 1948, one month after Israel was restored as a nation, continuing until 1955. The revival reached its peak after many of the participating ministers began building television ministries and pastoring large churches while only a handful continued their traveling ministry. One of the most noted ministers was William Branham. His ministry bordered on the spectacular. He was known for operating in the gifts of the Spirit: words of knowledge, miracles, and gifts of healing. While I never knew him personally, I have spoken to countless ministers who, during the Healing Revival, were young, sitting under Branham's ministry, or knew him personally. Not one minister who knew or heard him that I have met has ever spoken negatively of the man and often relates stories of his accuracy in every prophetic word he ever spoke.

In 1933, Branham was a twenty-five-year-old young minister. He had rented a facility and was conducting a revival. He wrote that he had just purchased a new Ford automobile. Sitting in the car, he suddenly felt the Spirit of God overwhelm him and went into, what he called, a "trance." This is a spiritual state required for seeing a vision while you are awake. The vision consisted of seven different events, one after the other, that would occur in the future. He saw all seven, wrote the information down on yellow paper, and placed it in his Bible. Through the years, from the 1950s into the early 1960s, when he publicly preached, he would occasionally bring up the 1933-vision, emphasizing the last four parts.

THE THREE "-ISMS"

In 1933, Hitler was rising in Germany. In the vision, Branham was told there would be three great "-isms" impacting the world: Communism, Fascism, and Nazism. In retrospect, all of the -isms brought war, death, and global chaos, emphasizing a loss of personal freedom while violently controlling the masses with their military forces. Today, we can sum up the desire to control information, money, and religion as the new form of Globalism where a few have their hands in manipulating and dominating the currency market, banking, food supply, transportation, and communications. This control is sealed by passing legislation that protects dictatorial powers and binds the mouths and hands of the common people.

In the first half of Branham's vision, he saw several major events that involved a coming war, involving President Roosevelt, Germany, and Hitler. In the vision, he also saw the rise of the Italian dictator, Mussolini, and his future invasion of Northern Africa, which did occur on October 3, 1935.

THE STRANGE CARS

The latter part of the vision was clear but quite puzzling to him. When retelling the vision in 1956, and several times thereafter, he wrote, *"Just before that time comes, automobiles will look like an egg"* (they were all a rectangle shape in 1933). He said, *"that's the way they will be just before the Rapture..."* When he saw these future cars, he also observed something that seemed completely impossible at the time of the vision. Again, he wrote, *"It will come to pass that cars will not be run by a steering wheel. Something else will run them (like a remote control). You can't hit another car because it is remote."* He continued to give details:

> *"I saw a family driving an automobile that was glass-topped and it didn't have a steering wheel. It was controlled by some kind of radar or something. People were playing games while it was driving itself...."*

Several points should be made. From the beginning of the automobile industry, especially from the 1920s through the 1990s, the shape of most cars was rectangular. However, at this present time, there are "12 cars shaped like an egg," engineered by Audi, Ford, Honda, Nissan,

Mazda, and Mitsubishi.[1] There are several small one-person vehicles that look like an egg on wheels. Modern vehicles have been designed for economical, ecological reasons, changing their shapes and sizes.

The second observation is a car that was driving itself and could not hit another car. For several years, automakers have worked to perfect a *driverless car.* These types of vehicles now exist. They have been tested and are in use. It was reported on marketplace.org, and I quote:

> *"This week, Cruise Automation, the self-driving car subsidiary of GM, introduced Origin, a fully autonomous vehicle that has no driving controls whatsoever. It's meant to be a rolling pod that carries passengers on demand, almost like a small bus or train car."*[2]

The first prototype "driverless" automobile was made in 1939 (7 years after this vision) and placed on exhibit at the New York World's Fair. The idea included an automated highway, using metal spikes to guide the self-driving vehicles. Over twenty years later, General Motors has developed a vehicle with sensors that could detect a wire in the road. In 1977, the Japanese engineered cameras that projected images from the road to assist in driving itself up to 56 MPH. It is predicted that by 2025, up to half of the road vehicles will be self-driving or autonomous.[3]

Our ministry has two travel SUVs that have a special setting, enabling the vehicles to stay between the lines on the road without the *driver* using the steering wheel. Some cars have computer technology that self-parks the vehicle. Some advanced models feature screens on the back headrests for viewing DVDs or playing games, just as Branham saw in his 1933 vision. However, the most interesting aspects of what he saw are the final two predictions.

A WOMAN AS PRESIDENT

After seeing the cars shaped in the form of an egg and driverless vehicles without a steering wheel, Branham then clearly saw the rise of a woman in the United States as the President. Below are the quotes from a compilation of sermons taken from his reel-to-reel messages:

> *"America will become ruled by a woman..."*
>
> *"A woman will take the place of a president of something of great high power in America."*
>
> *"I predict before the coming of the Lord, a woman will arise to be the leader..."*
>
> *"I saw a woman will either be president or come to some great power of some sort in the United States before the annihilation of the world..."*
>
> *"I saw a great woman raise up in the United States, well dressed and beautiful, but cruel in her heart. She will either guide or lead this nation to ruin (later, he used the word 'pollution')."*
>
> *"Remember, in the day before the end comes, that a woman... now you all keep all this wrote down. There will be a powerful woman raise up, either to be president, or dictator, or some great powerful woman in the United States; and she (America) will sink under the influence of a woman."* [4]

One year and five months prior to his death by an automobile accident (December 24, 1965), on July 26, 1964, during one of his recorded messages, Branham released a bold statement to reemphasize what he had been telling his audiences since 1933.

"The morals of our women are going to fall in such degraded things till they're going to be a disgrace to all nations...I saw a woman stand in the United States like a great queen or something. And she was beautiful to look at but wicked in her heart. She made America's step go with her step."

PRESIDENT HARRIS?

In the normal process, one would assume that this prediction indicates a woman will be voted in as president of the United States in a future election. However, there is another way. In 202I, the first female Vice President, Kamala Harris, was elected. Harris is a former Democratic Senator from California. In his sermons, Branham often indicated that a time would come when mostly women would be in charge of the nation, including the highest position.

Seldom does a sitting vice president become president. Out of 46 U.S. presidents in history, only eight vice presidents succeeded to the next office after the death of a president. In more recent times, Lyndon Johnson was sworn in as President after Kennedy's assassination in 1963, and Gerald Ford became President after Richard Nixon resigned in 1974. There has not been a woman president or vice president until now.

It is no secret that many public and private discussions have ensued concerning the physical health of Joe Biden. This is the first time since Branham's prophetic word (in 1933) that there is a possibility the vice-president, a woman, could be sworn in as the president of the United States. Between now and the end of 2024, due to Biden's health and other types of political issues, time will tell if this is the moment of fulfillment. If Biden passes, steps aside, or is somehow removed, with the way the political system is run, not only would Harris replace him, she would likely be tapped to run for president in 2024.

If Harris or another female fulfills this prophecy, it is not the fact that she is a *woman* that causes the conflict, as women were leaders and prophetesses in the Scripture (Exod. 15:20; Judg. 4:4; Neh. 6:14). Many women, such as the Queens of England, have served the British monarchy for centuries. It is the *extremist views* that certain women, baptized in the tub of radical socialism along with the new oppressive laws projected to be passed, will open the crater of a political volcano. With Harris, when political organizations examine her core values and beliefs, they are not just left but, they are extreme, including the costs of the "New Green Deal." An independent, nonpartisan website known as GovTrack called her the most liberal of 100 senators.[5] It will be time itself that will determine if this prophecy will unfold by 2024 or if it will be delayed for a future season.

THE LAST PART OF THE VISION

The final part of the vision is the most concerning part and takes place during the time this woman is in power. Here are the quotes taken from reel-to-reel magnet tape, later transcribed into print.

> *"Immediately after that, I saw the United States as one smoldering, burnt-over place (blown to bits). It was near the end."*

> *"I have seen, looked just like stumps burning, rocks blown out, and the whole United States just looked bare, laying like that, as far as I could see where I was standing."*[6]

To my knowledge, Branham never explained what would cause such massive destruction other than a possible invasion or an internal war. Let me add that there are dangerous fault lines, West Coast volcanos, and other natural disaster possibilities. A massive natural disaster could be another possible explanation for such burning and destruction. If not, then the two other choices are a foreign invasion or massive, violent in-state fighting. Branham believed this woman leader would be in office prior to the Rapture, although he made it clear that *the Lord didn't tell him that.* He just felt it in his spirit that it was possible.

Should Biden be forced to step down and Harris be placed in as the President, with the numerous biblical signs of the time of the end occurring, she could be the woman who fulfills Branham's vision. Should this not occur, I am one-hundred-percent confident that in the future, America will elect a woman president, not because the law of probability ensures this, but more importantly, those who personally knew Branham have said they never knew him to miss the mark on any of his visions, spiritual dreams, or words of knowledge. Some rejected his ministry due to doctrinal differences or the fact they did not believe in miraculous spiritual gifts. However, his accuracy cannot be challenged.

Based on the ideologies of Biden-Harris and the fact that his administration has surrounded themselves with not just progressives, but radical-left socialist-Marxist types, our patriots, freedom-defenders, and conservatives must not sit back and see the nation they love ruined by the hands of a few. These new liberal laws could result in the loss of our religious and social freedoms, including the registration of firearms, which could later be confiscated (as was the case with Hitler in Germany), arrests for hate-crimes, including preaching against certain sins, and passing a Green New Deal that eventually decimates the gas and oil industries. The clash is not coming—the clash is now here.

We must always keep in mind that all of the end-time biblical prophecies will come to pass. Some paint a very bleak picture. However, at the end of the end, the kingdom of God will rule for a thousand years (Rev. 20:4). However, since we are still on this planet with our future freedoms at stake, we must fight to keep our spiritual flames burning and our mouths open to free speech and expression.

CHAPTER 10

THE RISE OF THE TRUMP STUMP

Beginning with the election of Bill Clinton (1992) through 2016 with the election of Donald Trump, I received divine insight about each presidents' administration based on prophetic patterns prior to the election. When the presidential-voting controversy (2000) spread across the nation, using Old Testament patterns and by translating the names of Bush and Gore into the Hebrew language, interpreting the value of the individual Hebrew letters, I publicly predicted that Bush would win the election. It took weeks for the Florida recount to eventually be settled by the Supreme Court. In the year 2020, many who follow my ministry began inquiring what I was sensing for the 2020 election. The answer was, "absolutely nothing." There were numerous ministers, mostly on the internet, predicting, weeks and months in advance, a Trump victory. Some indicated a battle would ensue before and after. Personally, I saw no pattern, nor did I receive any inspiration concerning the outcome.

Over 70 million voters hoped Trump would serve a second term. Not because of his personality or (often) brazen comments, but because his legislation was often aligned with biblical values, and his negotiations on new agreements were having a positive impact on the economy, bringing a renewed spirit of hope to many people. He appointed hundreds of constitutional judges, including three in the Supreme Court who leaned conservative. He defended the life of the unborn. With the stroke of a pen, he moved the U.S. Embassy to Jerusalem and afterward initiated a peace plan for the Middle East, resulting in many Arab nations signing peace agreements with Israel. Before COVID, the economy was on fire, and employment for America's ethnic groups was at its highest. He passed a law giving prisoners a second chance. During his administration, he built a wall to protect the southern border. It was clear he was putting America first.

Despite denials from the secular media and numerous legislators, there was abundant evidence of voter fraud. I will not rehash evidence and not spend time attempting to prove this point. The end result was the swearing-in of Joe Biden, a long-time Washington insider.

PATTERNS EXPLAINING WHY

Many conservatives, including Christians and true patriotic Americans, were frustrated that there were no investigations into the voter inconsistencies, including states counting the votes of dead people. At the same time, those who are biblically informed are aware of Daniel's statement, "He (God) changes times and seasons: He removes kings and sets up kings" (Dan. 2:21). For months, I meditated on why, from God's perspective, the election went the direction it did and searched various scriptures for a previous historical pattern that could match the events we saw. After much searching, I believe I found a biblical parallel, which may also hold a *possible* pattern for the future. This information is not a "word from the Lord" but is a pattern.

BABYLON AND NEBUCHADNEZZAR

As I have written, the patterns of ancient Babel and Babylon are currently converging in America and the world. Nimrod represents the politics of control, globalism, and dictatorial powers. In the Babel system, the true God is rejected, as men viewed themselves as little gods. However, King Nebuchadnezzar put Babylon first, making his empire the envy of the world. He was known as "the greatest king of the Neo-Babylonian Empire. He is known for rebuilding much of Babylon and restoring it to its former glory."[1]

Although Nebuchadnezzar was not considered a "religious" man, he surrounded himself with an inner-circle of a few strong-Jewish believers, chiefly Daniel. This ancient king was an expert on money and economics and a master of international trade, permitting four young Jewish men access to his administration. The entire world was afraid of his armies, as the king would use them to stop any rebellion or uprising.

Nebuchadnezzar was the "Trump" of his day. Both men built an *empire.* Before becoming President, Donald Trump had built the *Trump Empire,* which included 13 five-star hotels, 17 golf courses in America and abroad, with real estate deals worth $823.3 million.[2] Trump's main office complex in New York called *"Trump Towers"* is a 58-floor, 644-foot-tall skyscraper, serving as the headquarters for the Trump organization. As president, using business principles and leverage, he canceled bad trade deals and rewrote them to help benefit America. He was the first U.S. President to challenge China in a trade war. His son-in-law, Jared Kushner, who is *Jewish,* sat with Trump during closed-door meetings as an advisor to the President. Jarod's grandparents were Holocaust survivors that moved to the United States in 1949. Jared was the primary negotiator for the Middle East agreements. He would be similar to Daniel in the Nebuchadnezzar story. In Babylon, Daniel had *three*-male Jewish companions (Dan. 2:17). Jared and Ivanka (Trump's daughter) have *three* children.

In the midst of Nebuchadnezzar's rule, the king was given a troubling dream while he was "flourishing (prospering) in his palace" (Dan. 4:4-5). In the dream, he saw a tree of great height, strong and visible to all on the earth. Everyone was prospering and enjoyed the shade and fruit of the tree. Suddenly, without warning, a great angel came down to earth saying, "cut down the tree, shake the leaves, and scatter the fruit" (Dan. 4:14). The cutting and shaking were so severe it caused the beasts of the field (other smaller nations) to flee from the tree. The angel then demanded that the stump and the roots remain in the earth (Dan. 4:15).

Daniel interpreted the meaning. The large, fruitful tree represented the king. He had grown great in the earth, successful in all he did, and his political decisions were impacting the entire earth. However, there was a high level of pride in which he felt his business ability was the sole source of this prosperity. What would occur to the king would separate him from his kingdom and humble him, creating an opportunity for an amazing restoration that would follow years later.

Here is Daniel's interpretation which occurred one year later:

- Daniel predicted "the king's tree would be cut down" – (Dan. 4:23)
- Daniel predicted "they would drive the king from men" – (Dan. 4:25)
- Daniel said, "the stump and root will remain in the earth" – (Dan. 4:26)

Daniel revealed that this event would demonstrate that God actually reigns over all nations, and He has the power to place anyone, even the "basest" (or lowest) of men, in positions of authority (Dan. 4:17). Daniel's instruction to Nebuchadnezzar was that if he would humble himself and repent before God, he would extend his rule and give the king tranquility. This included "showing mercy to the poor," which apparently was one of the sins of Nebuchadnezzar (Dan. 4:27). Here is what occurred twelve months later:

> *"All this came upon King Nebuchadnezzar. At the end of the twelve months, he was walking about the royal palace of Babylon. The king spoke, saying, 'Is not this great Babylon, that I have built for a royal dwelling by my mighty power and for the honor of my majesty?' While the word was still in the king's mouth, a voice fell from heaven: 'King Nebuchadnezzar, to you it is spoken: the kingdom has departed from you! And they shall drive you from men...'"*
>
> – DANIEL. 4:28-32 (NKJV)

For seven years, the king was out of power. However, at the end of this test, God allowed him to return to the original position as the Babylonian King. The severe trial had changed his perception of himself and of God. The king completely turned his heart and life over to the God of Daniel, the only true God. After returning to his palace, the king wrote:

> *"For His dominion is an everlasting dominion, and His kingdom is from generation to generation. All the inhabitants of the earth are reputed as nothing; He does according to His will in the army of heaven. And among the inhabitants of the earth. No one can restrain His hand, or say to Him, "What have You done?"*
>
> – DANIEL 4:34-35 (NKJV)

Months following the election, many have asked, "What is God doing?" "Why were our prayers not answered?" Nebuchadnezzar discovered that God alone does what He desires with a purpose that is concealed but revealed much later. This is true with the rise and removal of world leaders.

In the king's dream, the tree's stump and roots remained firm in the earth. This imagery indicated that despite the king losing his position, his kingdom and his administration, after several years, would grow back, and he would return to lead again. After a great humiliation and separation from his position, God favored the former king to be restored as a future king.

MEN SEEK HUMILIATION—GOD SEEKS HUMILITY

The definition of *humility* is "a modest or low view of one's own importance." Nebuchadnezzar was a born visionary. He spent many years constructing massive edifices and strategizing economic success. However, he never really gave God the glory. While standing at his palace balcony, he was bragging on himself, saying "I" and "my" (see Dan. 4:28-30). It is difficult for any world leader, highly successful billionaire businessmen, corporate CEOs, and well-known politicians to exercise true humility. This is because humility is often perceived by strong personalities as a weakness. Man's pre-conceived idea is that if I am a humble person, everyone will think I am weak and take advantage of me. The U.S. military knows that America must be perceived as strong to remain strong in the eyes of her enemies. If a president spoke of some tragedy with tears in his eyes, his media enemies would take a jab at him and imply he was breaking down and showing weakness. Compassion and weakness are different. He was expressing compassion, which arrogant people know nothing about.

One important key is to *"Be humble before God and be strong before men."* It is what we do in *secret* that impacts what we become in *public*. The scripture teaches that pride produces contention (Prov. 13:10), and with pride comes shame (Prov. 11:2). The wise King Solomon wrote that "Pride goes before destruction, and a haughty spirit before a fall" (Prov. 16:18). The Scripture teaches, "…he that humbles himself shall be exalted" (Matt. 23:12). James revealed, "Humble yourself in the sight of God and he shall lift you up" (James 4:10). Peter also penned that the humble would eventually be exalted (1 Pet. 5:6). From the view of the Almighty, "God resists the proud, and gives grace to the humble" (1 Pet. 5:5). The word "grace" also alludes to "favor." Humility includes the ability to admit when you have done wrong or made a wrong decision. David committed a horrible iniquity that should have sentenced him to execution by stoning. However, when confronted by a prophet, he immediately admitted his sins and sought God's forgiveness. His humility touched God's heart, who, in return, carried David through some very distressing times.

HOW DOES THIS PATTERN FIT TRUMP?

Using the parallels of Nebuchadnezzar, after *rebuilding* the American economy, Trump experienced the same types of separations from not only the presidency but from people attempting to economically destroy his "Trump Empire." First, despite mounting evidence of voting inconsistencies and state rules being changed illegally, he was forced (*driven*) from his position of leadership. Just as the ancient king's tree was cut down, destroying the branches, leaves, and fruit, Trump was humiliated with a second impeachment from the House of Representatives, "cut off" from all social media, with numerous attempts by his enemies to "cut off" his business income. Just like Nebuchadnezzar, many people enjoyed the fruit of the "king's" tree, sitting in the shade when all was going well, yet began fleeing from him when they saw the tree falling to the ground. They ran for cover. As most social media banned Trump, many of those who stood with him were suddenly running away, making negative public statements to protect their own political futures to avoid media criticism.

In Trump's situation, he and his legal team saw over 100 lawsuits filed against election fraud thrown out. He was banned from posting on most major social media sites. Some of his bank accounts were canceled, and pressure was put on publishers not to publish his future books. The second impeachment was an attempt to prevent him from ever running for public office again. This was in an effort to completely stop all influence. On Biden's first day in office, he reversed numerous Executive Orders Trump had signed, which was reported by the media as "the end of Trump's legacy." In the days after his departure, polls rating Trump's approval were rigged to question twenty percent more Democrats to present a false percentage indicating that Trump had the lowest ratings when leaving office than any president in history. However, the respected and more accurate Rasmussen tracking poll indicated Trump departed with a 51% approval rating.[3] Thus, the roots and the stump of the tree remained.

WILL THE TREE RETURN?

America's radical and leftist-progressive politicians are literally terrified of the *pro-American movement* formed by Donald Trump's organization. Over half of America supports America First, along with the civil, religious, and free speech rights guaranteed in the Constitution, and defending our God-given freedoms. Trump was not a globalist but a patriotic American businessman. The Deep State, including the Harvard-Yale-good-old-boys club, mixed with the billionaire globalists, felt resistance coming from massive crowds of flag-waving patriotic Americans. They have done everything in their power to "cut him down" and make the movement irrelevant.

However, if the Nebuchadnezzar parallels are a historical reflection, paralleling Donald Trump, then the *Trump stump* and roots are deep in the soil of America, and with time, humility, and wisdom, he will either return to an important position, form a new political party, or watch as a new tree will grow out of the Trump stump. The new tree may not involve him personally but may include other members of his family.

In America's history, family-political legacies are common. America's most recognized political family is the Kennedys. They influenced American politics for sixty years. One Kennedy, in 1960, John F. Kennedy, became president of the United States. Other brothers and their children served in the Senate or political offices on national, state, and local levels. At least thirteen Kennedy's have served in high-level political positions. Most political analysts believe the Kennedy legacy came to a close when Joe Kennedy conceded a defeat to his political opponent in 2020.

If Trump himself cannot (because of impeachment rules, health, or other reasons, or if he chooses not to) run for president, the fact remains, he has become the face and voice of a new movement, unlike anything I have witnessed in my lifetime. There are an estimated 74 million voters who cast ballots for Trump. Many believe there was election-corruption and, at the least, illegal manipulation against President Trump in five battleground states. Most people I have spoken with are willing to "stump" (speak up) for a pro-Constitutional movement.

THE UNSEEN FROM GOD'S PERSPECTIVE

The world and the United States have entered a season of prophetic alignment and fulfillment. Seasons of prophetic fulfillment have a dual track. One track is the light of the Gospel shining God's truth around the world with the outpouring of the Holy Spirit (Matt. 24:14;

Joel 2:28-29). The opposite track is the train of apostasy, with boxcars marked perilous times, violence, natural disasters, corruption, and evil, steamrolling its way through towns and cities. These two opposing forces of light and darkness are headed for a showdown, unseen in modern times. The opposing sides in this boxing ring for freedom will be, in one corner, the radical-left, facing off against the conservative-right in the other corner. It will look like Christians debating Atheists, love versus anger, light against darkness, and good against evil.

We know who wins in the end. However, there will be a battle to remain standing without throwing in the towel, to finish strong when the bell rings at the end of the twelfth round.

THE UNKNOW IS OUT THERE

Each United States President faced one or several major crises that tested his strength, wisdom, and loyalty to the Constitution. With Kennedy, it was the 1962 Cuban missile crisis. Nixon's Waterloo was the Watergate break-in, leading to his impeachment in 1973. Regan participated in the fall of Communism, secretly providing assistance for anti-Communist uprisings in Eastern Europe. For Herbert Walker Bush, in 1990-91, he dealt with a sudden Gulf War. During Bill Clintons eight years, his conflicts included numerous personal crises mingled with terrorist attacks on American interests in 1998. George W. Bush, America's forty-third President, was serving during the tragic 9-11 attacks that lead America into a new global war on terrorism. President Obama, in eight years, had little success in getting the economy on track. For Trump, his battle was with the deep-state corrupt politicians and avoiding getting devoured by the alligators in the D.C. swamp.

Herein is the unknown. What unforeseen disaster or national crisis will President Joe Biden or possibly President Kamala Harris experience between now and November 2024? Based on scientific evidence, there is a high probability that they will see several noted global or national natural disasters. There are warnings of a serious economic crisis impacting America or nations throughout the world. Parts of their "save the planet" agenda are projected to cost millions of jobs and trillions of dollars. There is a ghost of the 1929 economic depression walking the halls of Congress that could manifest once again.

In the Old Testament, when God desired to chastise Israel for breaking His Commandments, *He did so by allowing bad, immoral, corrupt, and oppressive kings to take power.* These egotistical leaders created economic and religious chaos, sending the common people in Israel to their knees, crying out to God for mercy and deliverance. The same happens when Americans choose a progressive who passes laws that legalize abominations. Grieving Christians fall to their knees, cry out to God, and show up in masses to vote. The cycle of the left-hand versus the right-hand repeats, just as it did with good kings and not-so-good kings in Israel thousands of years ago.

When "bad leaders" control the legislation decision-making in Washington, D.C., the entire nation will feel the impact. Just as in ancient Israel, we can experience *economic chastisement.* This national chastisement was evident as a result of Israel selecting Saul as their first king. The people received the man they wanted to lead the nation, but over time, they didn't like what they got. Saul's leadership style and careless raising of taxes and other wrong choices impacted the people to be "discontent, discouraged, and in debt" (1 Sam. 22:2). Saul became obsessed with removing David from any future possibility of becoming Israel's king. Saul transitioned from being an anointed leader to one tormented by evil spirits (1 Sam. 16:14-16).

American patriotism is a wonderful thing. Becoming a citizen of the Kingdom of God, through a redemptive covenant, is a far better thing! For starters, the retirement plan includes eternal life and the rule of all kingdoms on earth in the future. Time is the revealer of prophetic patterns, cycles, and direct biblical fulfillment. The details found in numerous Old Testament stories often conceal events that will repeat. With the world moving toward a Babylonian form of globalism, the major activities that unfolded in Babel and Babylon will repeat in the future. The Daniel 4 narrative seems to hold many parallel events in the life of Nebuchadnezzar and Trump. *The tree, the stump, and the return of Trump could one day be a pattern we will see.* If not, the stump of a pro-Constitution movement is now rooted in American soil.

CHAPTER 11

HOW CAN THE PROPHETS GET IT WRONG?

Does the Lord still speak to individuals today? If so, how is this accomplished? Can a person who claims to be expressing some type of "revelation," saying God has given them specific information, end up "missing it? If so, did the person claiming to be a "prophet" or "prophetess" actually hear from the Lord? These types of questions have been posed when men and women have said, "God told me this would happen," then it did not happen.

The New Testament indicates there are nine spiritual gifts (1 Cor. 12:7-10). There are three schools of thought concerning the present-day operation of these nine gifts. The first being the total *cessation* of all nine gifts. This theory states that the nine gifts, called the *charismata* in Greek, were initiated on the Day of Pentecost (Acts 2:1-4), continuing throughout the ministry of the twelve original Apostles. Those believing in cessation explain that after the last Apostle's death (the Apostle John) around AD 100, the nine spiritual gifts ceased operating in the church as they were only necessary during the first century to assist in confirming the message of the Apostles.

The second school of thought teaches *partial cessation*, a theory explaining how certain spiritual gifts such as a word of wisdom, knowledge, and faith continue in the present church age. However, the miraculous gifts such as the working of miracles, healings, along with the vocal gift of tongues, interpretation, and prophecy, ceased with the completion of the New Testament. They base this ceasing on an exegesis of 1 Corinthians 13:8-10, where Paul wrote, "tongues shall cease."

The third group believes that all nine gifts are active today among Spirit-filled believers who earnestly seek after these gifts for the purpose of ministering to others. The majority within this group believe in the operation of three vocal gifts: tongues, interpretation of tongues, and prophecy. The gift of prophecy described as an "inspired utterance" can involve foretelling and forth telling. Said another way, this vocal gift can involve both preaching a message or declaring an inspired word from the Holy Spirit, including an element of predicting some future event or providing direction for someone.

I was raised with several noted ministers who operated in the gifts of the Spirit. Several times, on at least three occasions, I experienced dreams or visions with national implications that came to pass, in perfect detail, many years later. Twice, I publicly told congregations of a prophetic spiritual vision and dream I had years before it occurred. When the events happened, people remembered the revelation. At different moments in my father's sixty years of ministry, I personally saw God use him in many of these spiritual gifts.

ELECTION PREDICTIONS

Prior to the 2020 presidential election, those who "run in prophetic circles" began appearing on social media with dreams, visions, and alleged words from the Lord that Trump would win a second term. Every few days, another minister would make a prophetic announcement confirming the same. After November 3, it soon became clear that there were numerous inconsistencies, including voter fraud, in several battleground states Trump needed to win. Weeks later, many individual prophetic voices began saying they were correct, but the election was stolen. A few took the proper and biblical method of saying they had misinterpreted a dream or had perhaps spoken out of their own spirit.

My father often said, "the gifts are flawless, but the vessels are not." As an example, one moment, Simon Peter received a revelation that Jesus was the Son of God. A few verses later, Jesus rebuked Peter for listening to the voice of Satan. He went from a revelation to a rebuke. The first voice was God speaking to him and the second comment was him speaking from the wrong source (Matt. 16:16-23). If someone misses their prediction, it does not mean they were deceived, a false prophet, or heard from Satan. However, there are some lessons to learn when giving what you believe is a word from God.

The first is the danger of the seduction of fame. Long before I hosted weekly teachings on television called Manna-Fest, I was told by an older, more experienced minister that television could make a minister appear "smarter than he actually is, or dumber than they actually are." On any form of visual media, a person must find their message and the method of delivery. Christians of all denominational backgrounds seek out different subjects from a biblical viewpoint that appeal to them. This can create a loyal viewing audience. However, watching your numbers rise on a social media channel or hearing people compliment your teaching can be dangerous for, what Paul termed, a "novice" (1 Tim. 3:6), which refers to something "newly planted" or someone inexperienced.

A true spiritual dream, vision, or Word from God cannot lie and will come to pass. In 1988, I experienced a full-color vision with specific instruction. From that point, my messages were centered on Bible prophecy, including teaching Christians about our Hebraic roots, connecting our spiritual parallels and patterns with Israel, the land, ancient history, and the Jewish people. When our program launched on television in the year 2000, the prophetic emphasis began reaching a large audience. Programs included eight months of telecasts taped on-location in Israel. These programs were often the highest viewed programs on several networks.

INTERNET PROPHETS

With the introduction of social media platforms such as YouTube, anyone can create a channel and, within months or a few years, link with people from around the world, keeping up with their information. This is a positive feature if a minister is sincere, desiring to bring an important Bible message or a "right now" truth to a targeted audience. However, it can also give individuals that are not seasoned in ministry, in scripture, or have little or no ministry accountability a platform in which to *call themselves* a "prophet or a prophetess." Because of these titles, some gullible Christians believe every word they speak must be genuine.

THE BIGGEST DANGER

I say this not as a critic but out of concern. Being a "social-media prophet" comes with the danger of weaker, baby Christians treating their messages as they would a secular psychic, looking every day for some personal or national word of direction. The biggest danger is people neglecting to read and study the Bible, replacing valuable, personal, intimate study time for a quick word from God. The Bible is the most accurate source of future events. At times, a person may receive a word of wisdom or a word of knowledge, and people call the warning or instruction a "prophetic word."

I once heard a great minister, Lester Sumrall, make a rather controversial but true statement. He explained that he was not a fan of "personal prophecy," although he did believe that a personal, prophetic word would basically confirm something you already knew and should be used more as "confirmation." Then he said something that made sense. He said, "So many people are running around asking someone who is anointed to give them a word from the Lord, or they ask them if they have a prophecy for them." Lester commented, "If a person is close to God in prayer, He will tell them what they need to know. The reason people always want a word is because *they* are not praying!"

My own father, Fred Stone, was so accurate in a word of knowledge, being warned by the Holy Spirit of future events, that during his latter years, when he traveled with me, I never recall him missing it or being proven wrong. He saw terrorist plans with warnings so accurate that he had the audience of the F.B.I. when he had a dream or a vision. He had similar gifts like Jacob, Joseph, and Daniel in dreams and interpretations. Growing up, it was impossible for any of us kids to sin or do wrong, as he would dream of what we were doing, later confronting us.

Those who knew my father acknowledged he operated in the gift of prophecy. Several fellow ministers and people sitting under his ministry called him a "prophet." This is because of the many warnings he received that proved to be accurate. However, Dad would never, under any condition, call himself a prophet. He would simply say, "The Lord has blessed me with His gifts."

INTERPRETING A WORD FROM HEAVEN

When it comes to dreams, not every dream or alleged vision comes from the Lord. At times, we can have strange dreams because of what we eat, because we're restless, or perhaps our spirit is troubled.

In the Old Testament era, there were many men calling themselves prophets. Some were scattered throughout the tribes of Israel. Others were hanging out at the tabernacle (later the temple), mingling with priests in Jerusalem. Ancient kings often staffed their administration with their own personal prophets or wise men, hoping they were inspired to interpret cosmic activity, the meaning of a troubling dream, or inquire of the Lord (if the men were Hebrew prophets) for His direction or purpose.

On two occasions, all of the wise men hired by Nebuchadnezzar were unable to interpret the king's dream or visions. When Daniel was called to the king's throne, in both instances, he alone gave the correct interpretations. The same was true when Joseph was led from an Egyptian prison to interpret Pharaoh's two dreams, warning of a future seven-year famine. Dreaming and correctly interpreting is a special gift from the Holy Spirit. Dreams from God can only be interpreted by a true servant of God, as proven with Joseph and Daniel.

DUELING PROPHETS

What happens when two prophecies oppose one another? In Jerusalem, Jeremiah encountered a serious clash with dueling prophetic words. The majority of Jerusalem's "prophets" were spreading stories of their own dreams that were opposite of Jeremiah's warnings. Jeremiah was predicting that a violent and destructive invasion by the Babylonians was coming, targeting Jerusalem and the sacred temple. Among most priests, elders, and temple prophets, Jeremiah's words were considered negative, opening the door for spiritual leaders to continually reject his public words. The people were confused, not knowing which word—trouble coming or trouble avoided—was correct. Should they prepare for hard times or reject Jeremiah's warnings? Jeremiah was harsh on those who disagreed with his prophecies of a future Babylonian assault. He wrote:

"And the Lord said to me, "The prophets prophesy lies in My name. I have not sent them, commanded them, nor spoken to them; they prophesy to you a false vision, divination, a worthless thing, and the deceit of their heart."

– Jeremiah 14:14

"I have heard what the prophets have said who prophesy lies in My name, saying, 'I have dreamed, I have dreamed!' How long will this be in the heart of the prophets who prophesy lies? Indeed, they are prophets of the deceit of their own heart."

– Jeremiah 23:25-26

Apparently, these temple prophets had given accurate words in the past, or they would not have been called "prophets." However, the warnings of Jeremiah, at the time, were not matching the cities prosperity. In the end, the majority of Jerusalem's prophets got it wrong, and one lonely man, Jeremiah, hit the mark. True prophets were not popular.

MOSES' INSTRUCTION

There were idol temples in Egypt operating with an active priesthood who worked along-side *seers* that would read from cups and explore the veins in animal livers. They would tap into bizarre methods attempting to reveal future events. The Egyptians were familiar with dream interpretations. Moses, who was adopted by Pharaoh's daughter, grew up in Pharaoh's house rubbing shoulders with so-called wise men, magicians, idol priests, and dream interpreters. Moses wrote:

"Then He said, 'Hear now My words: If there is a prophet among you, I the Lord, make Myself known to him in a vision; I speak to him in a dream.'"

– Numbers 12:6 (NKJV)

Ancient people and previous empires were in tune with the spirit world, often crossing from the light of God to the darkness of evil. Moses witnessed the false and the real clash when his rod was transformed into a serpent, and two Egyptian magicians mimicked the same miracle. It is always important to separate the true from the false. When it came to prophets, Moses was instructed by the Lord to write:

> *"If there arises among you a prophet or a dreamer of dreams, and he gives you a sign or a wonder, and the sign or the wonder comes to pass, of which he spoke to you, saying, 'Let us go after other gods'—which you have not known—'and let us serve them,' you shall not listen to the words of that prophet or that dreamer of dreams, for the Lord your God is testing you to know whether you love the Lord your God with all your heart and with all your soul."*
>
> – Deuteronomy 13:1-3 NKJV

Moses wanted the people to take note of the prophet's doctrine and not the prophet's dream. The right dream with the wrong teaching is a false teacher.

WHAT WOULD PAUL DO?

Paul gives the Body of Christ the best example of how to discern a "word from the Lord" that a minister is presenting. He teaches how to separate what is a "word from the Lord" versus the *opinion* of the minister. Paul explained, in 1 Corinthians 14:6, the four methods of communicating spiritual truth. He wrote:

> *"...What shall I profit you, except I shall speak to you either by revelation, or by knowledge, or by prophesying, or by doctrine?"*

The first method is a direct *revelation* from the Lord. In 2 Corinthians 12:1, Paul pointed out that he received "visions and revelations from the Lord." On one occasion, he was "caught up to the third heaven, into paradise," where he saw unspeakable secrets (2 Cor. 12:4). Scholars believe that God revealed to Paul seven distinct revelations that no one before him had received, including the New Testament revelation of the coming of the Lord for the church (1 Thess. 4:16-18). Paul's writings indicated God made known to him revelations kept secret from the foundation of the world (Eph. 3:9).

The second method of releasing spiritual information is through knowledge. This is truth already made known through personal study of the Torah, the prophets, or in Paul's day, the Old Testament scriptures. Ministers and teachers who instruct in scriptural knowledge gain insights that become volumes of knowledge for others, as these truths can be taught when applied on a practical level.

A third method is mentioned when Paul wrote instructions to the church (about the physical relationship between a husband and wife) that were not directly from the Lord. He introduced his comments by saying, "But I speak this by permission, and not of commandment" (1 Cor. 7:6). This statement explains that Paul's comments were written after much *prayer*, receiving a *release* within his spirit, and were not a direct commandment from the Lord. The fourth method is speaking by doctrine, a teaching which was established using the words of Christ and the Apostles, which, in Paul's day, was known and also being revealed.

HOW TO PRESENT A WORD FROM THE LORD

Both Joel 2 and Acts 2 indicate that in the final last-day outpouring of the Spirit, old men will dream dreams, and young men shall see visions. The Bible makes it clear that a person can experience a dream or vision, claiming it is from the Lord, when in reality, it may be something from their own spirit. Often in a true spiritual dream, there is unusually symbolism requiring an interpretation, comparing it with symbolism found in the Bible.

In my sincere opinion, there are far too many that have taken on the title of prophet or prophetess, saying, "God told me," or, "The Lord said," *so often* that it's almost more of a habit to confirm their title. When a person's word is trusted, what follows, "God told me," is a very serious statement that carries eternal weight. When a man or woman "releases a prophetic revelation from the Lord," and their dream, vision, or word clearly does not come to pass, it causes weak believers to become disillusioned and doubtful, and mature Christians to become cynical. The same is true if a minister experiences some form of personal or ministry failure.

This is what my wise father taught me. He said, "If I believe I have a word in my spirit from the Holy Spirit, but I am not certain, then I must "try the spirits" (1 John 4:1), meaning test it to see if it is your spirit or the Holy Spirit. He said, "To do this, if you are uncertain, tell the congregation, 'I am sensing something in my spirit and am not sure it is the Lord, so I am going to reveal it and if it is for someone here, then either raise your hand or come forward and then we will know the Lord is directing the word.'" When I sense a word of knowledge or wisdom in my spirit, and say, "I am testing this to see if this is from the Lord," the majority of the time a person acknowledges the word was accurate and for them.

Paul provided a series of rules when someone was speaking a prophetic word in the church.

"Let two or three prophets speak, and let the others judge. But if anything is revealed to another who sits by, let the first keep silent. For you can all prophesy one by one, that all may learn and all may be encouraged. And the spirits of the prophets are subject to the prophets. For God is not the author of confusion but of peace, as in all the churches of the saints."

– 1 Corinthians 14:29-33

The Greek word here for judge means "to separate thoroughly, to oppose, to differ." It is the same method a judge uses in court to hear evidence. They take each part — piece by piece — and look closer at what was presented. It is not for the purpose of nit-picking to find some fault, but to see if the word aligns with sound teaching, biblical doctrine, and good common sense! If the mature elders believe the correct criterion was not met, they have the right to say, "This word is not correct."

RESPONDING TO A "MISSED WORD"

It is quite provoking and confusing when a detailed prediction is missed, and the person attempts to by-pass responsibility. It is always disheartening when the world begins to mock spiritual gifts because something someone said never happened. Another issue is the attitude of the individual who is claiming or operating in the gifts, especially in the vocal gifts. The church at Corinth featured the gifts of tongues, interpretation, and prophecy. However, there was much confusion. Paul wrote an entire chapter to correct the abuse that was causing division (1 Cor. 14).

Anyone who believes they are operating in a gift of the Spirit must use discretion and exercise wisdom on how the message is presented. When John wrote the book of Revelation, the Lord warned against "adding to and taking away" from the words in the book (Rev. 22:18).

God treated the "taking away" from His word so seriously that John wrote, "If any man shall take away from the words of the book of this prophecy, God shall take away his part out of the book of life, and out of the holy city…" (Rev. 22:19). When presenting a prophetic word under divine inspiration, it is important not to add more than the Spirit of the Lord is giving.

A person's test that they are moving in a true prophetic anointing is not because of a title placed upon your name. Neither is it one dream you have that was accurate. It is not based upon your ability to cry out, "Thus saith the Lord." It is based upon a true calling and accuracy. When someone asked me, "What do you think about that prophetic word," my answer is always, "I'll tell you if or when it comes to pass." The Holy Spirit is a spirit of truth and does not manipulate our faith or emotions through prophetic words. God is not the author of confusion. A true word could be a warning. However, mixed messages will certainly confuse.

I was taught, and I continue to teach, that the first element a person should seek when asking God to use them in any of the spiritual gifts is *wisdom*. I have seen strangers show up at a church with a notebook and demand to get a microphone to give the congregation "a word from God." When told they cannot just get up and give a word without first giving the word to an elder, they blow-up, get-red faced, then announce doom and gloom on the church or ministry for rejecting their words. The person's lack of submission and humility, to them, is some twisted sign of their "prophetic boldness."

These situations remind me of when Christ was rejected by the Samaritans. James and John said, "wilt thou that we command fire to come down from heaven, and consume them?" The Jews had animosity—a sort of family feud—against the Samaritans, and seeing them destroyed (a sign of God's judgment) would have made some anti-Samaritan religious Jews in Jerusalem happy. Jesus responded to the challenge by rebuking these two disciples he had surnamed "sons of thunder" (Mark 3:17) by saying, "You do not know what manner of spirit you are of" (Luke 9:55).

Good shepherds guard their pulpits, and this includes protecting the sheep from a self-appointed and self-called man or woman who may be seeking affirmation or confirmation for a title they have given themselves. Gifts are to be used in wisdom, under the supervision of spiritual authority and must be judged by mature elders.

At the same time, we must be cautious not to "despise prophecy" (1 Thess. 5:20). If a man or woman says, "Thus saith the Lord," and it does not come to pass, God Himself is their judge, and He will chastise the person to correct them. It should be our goal to maintain unity in the Body of Christ and focus on the Bible. The scripture is always the most accurate and sure word that we can trust one hundred percent.

CHAPTER 12

SILICON VALLEY: THE LAND OF SAND

Having traveled to California numerous times, I clearly understand why so many people wish to live there. For starters, the weather is stable and warm throughout most of the year, and there are beautiful mountains, some with snow-capped ski resorts, beaches with palm trees waving in the breeze, and don't forget the Pacific Ocean. Let's not forget the malls are amazing, and the restaurants feature chefs from around the world creating tasty dishes, bringing a taste of the nations to every major city. Northern California is also the world's tech capital.

On the west coast of northern California, south of the San Francisco Bay, is the region called Silicon Valley, a name first used in 1971. The entire region is the global center for computer and phone technology. The cities in and around this area have the third-highest GDP per capita in the world.

Thirty technology companies throughout this area are listed on the Fortune 1,000 businesses. The valley hosts noted corporate names such as Apple, Cisco, eBay, Hewlett Packard, Lockheed Martin, Netflix, Twitter, Zoom, YouTube, and numerous lesser recognized names. Early on, the valley became known for specializing in *silicon-based* transistors (circuit chips). Today, Silicon Valley is known for developing software, internet, and computer systems.[1]

SAND LAND

Popular Science Magazine had this heading: *Making Silicon from Sand.* Underneath this magazine heading were the following words, "In a chemical reaction straight out of Harry Potter, you can turn dirt into the building block of every computer." Silicon is the key element in every computer processor. The earthly elements of rock, clay, and especially sand have various forms of silica. When properly heating common silica sand, the end product becomes elemental silicon.[2] Another interesting fact is most of the world's grains of sand contain quartz, which is also a form of silicon dioxide known as silica, a substance used for the chips in today's wireless phones.

THE STORY OF SAND

There is a very interesting statement that Christ made, affirming how *water* impacts rock and sand:

> *"Therefore whoever hears these sayings of Mine, and does them, I will liken him to a wise man who built his house on the rock: and the rain descended, the floods came, and the winds blew and beat on that house; and it did not fall, for it was founded on the rock. But everyone who hears these sayings of Mine, and does not do them, will be like a foolish man who built his house on the sand: and the rain descended, the floods came, and the winds blew and beat on that house; and it fell. And great was its fall."*
>
> – Matthew 7:24-27 (NKJV)

I do not wish to stretch some interpretation beyond its meaning. However, I want to present these passages with a modern application. The basic meaning is those building on the rock are constructing their lives on a solid foundation of truth, so strong, that storms and floods cannot destroy it. When Peter announced Christ was the Son of God, Christ promised, "Upon this rock I will build my church and the gates of hell will not prevail against it" (Matt. 16:18). The "rock" was the revelation that Christ was God's son. In Christ's statement, the sand is a weak foundation that will shift or wash away when floods of water siege their foundation. Building a life without Christ and His truth is building a sand palace.

Silicon Valley is an amazing region with some of the smartest scientists and researchers in the world making billions of dollars by dealing with a substance *found in sand* (as stated earlier). Constructing computer chips of all types requires silicon, the main substance in sand and quartz sand. Jesus explained a common fact, building with sand seems safe, that is until water is present and the storms strike. One wave on a beach will wipe out any sandcastle.

If you own an iPhone or a laptop, one substance is your primary threat: water. When you spill your Cola on your keyboard, it will destroy the chips and boards inside your personal computer. If you drop an average, non-waterproof iPhone accidentally in the toilet and the water reaches the interior, damage can occur. This is due to water causing corrosion when combining metal with oxygen, creating iron oxide. This iron oxide is commonly known as rust.[3]

Think about how billions of dollars of technology, continually being updated with new devices, controls, and impacts the world from one location in Northern California. Furthermore, the billions of dollars pouring into corporate bank accounts are created from a substance found in sand. Out of all of the earth's natural elements, sand is perhaps the most unstable as it can be relocated with the slightest *wind.*

The scripture warns of being "tossed to and frow, and carried about with every wind of doctrine" (Eph 4:14). Sand cannot resist nor can it remain in one place as when a wave from the sea washes over it, it is carried from land and lost in the ocean. James wrote that when we "waver" in our faith, we become like a wave of the sea, driven and tossed (James 1:6). Jude identified those who turn from Christ and compromise their faith as "raging waves and wandering stars" (Jude 13).

WHEN NATURE TURNS VIOLENT

There are many natural calamities that could very easily disrupt all forms of communication and computer technology, sending the modern world back to the 1800s.

- Solar flares that could knock out the power grid, disrupting any devices requiring electricity.
- Major earthquakes could destroy offices, although modern buildings have some retrofitting features.
- A Pacific tsunami of massive size could easily flood and destroy communications and offices.

The stunning and amazing technology we all require for daily living, including sending and receiving texts, e-mails, videos, and pictures, all with a click of a mouse or the push of one button, is basically built with sand. As Christ indicated, all it takes is a flood of water to shake a sand foundation.

VISIONS OF WHAT IS COMING

Scripture indicates that in the last days, prior to the return of Christ, men will be given spiritual dreams and visions (Joel 2:28-29) to reveal what is coming in the future, how to be prepared, and why certain things happen. At times, it may be years before a dream or a vision comes to pass. Pharaoh dreamt of a future seven-year famine. God allowed Joseph to have seven years to collect grain before allowing the horrible famine to strike the world. In 1996, I saw a vision of the World Trade Center shrouded in black, with five greyish tornadoes spinning off the building. I observed papers and other small objects within the grey, spinning clouds. Five years later, terrorists flew planes into the Twin Towers, collapsing both buildings, sending grey spinning clouds into the streets. I realized the vision I saw was occurring.

On several occasions, I have experienced detailed dreams of tsunamis with waves of huge heights rising in the ocean and smashing into cities on the western coast of the United States. In one vision, I was flying, and as soon as the plane was in the air, I could see a massive wave coming from the Pacific Ocean, preparing to hit a city where I had been ministering in California. Although it was a dream, I sensed the fear and anxiety the people were experiencing.

In another dream, an earthquake in the Pacific Ocean had shaken the entire West Coast. Suddenly, tsunami alarms went off. Several others and I got into a vehicle and headed toward the mountains. When we arrived, I was invited into a house. The family had watched my television program and recognized me. Water was rushing in at the base of the mountain. Her television was on, and a helicopter was presenting live footage on Fox-News. It was a devastating sight.

I am careful not to publicly speak of these types of warnings until I sense a release to do so. I am now sounding a trumpet of warning as in 2021, I began to sense a burden each time I thought about these dreams. As previously stated, at times, a dream or vision may take years to come to pass. When it comes to a natural disaster or a selective judgment, the Almighty always extends mercy on behalf of His covenant people.

HOW TO PREPARE?

At times, it has been extremely difficult for me to speak about what I have seen. With my past track record of seeing many things before they happened, people will ask, after I have seen destruction coming, if and when they should move. I cannot and do not answer that question. Just as God gave Noah and Lot a plan of escape, prior to a global (flood) and regional disaster (burning of Sodom), the Lord will direct His people to the right places at the right time.

If a family lives in a possible "target zone," including coastal areas subject to hurricanes, earthquakes, or a possible tsunami, there should be practical preparations in the event of a natural disaster. This includes water, food, methods of communication, and ways to recharge electrical devices. There are things we cannot control, including the selective and global judgments that will occur. It is not a lack of faith or mistrust in God to have a plan of action. Christ warned His followers that both the Temple and Jerusalem would be destroyed within one generation and the signs to look for prior to this happening. He told His followers to "flee to the mountains" (Luke 21:21).

It is the foundation made with "stone" that will endure the earth, wind, fire, and all forms of shaking that will strike. Our foundation is our redemptive covenant with Christ. Learning to pray and listen to the still small voice of our heavenly Father has always been the key to all favor and blessings.

CHAPTER 13

WHAT THE DEEP STATE DID TO MY FRIEND

For years, the use of the term "deep state" brought raised eyebrows and accusations of "on-the-fringe" conspiracy theories. The phrase "shadow government" was occasionally spoken when describing unknown individuals within various high-level agencies "pulling strings" to control a pre-determined outcome. More recently, the phrase "*deep state*" has been repeated countless times by conservative cable news commentators. The definition of "deep state" is "*a secret cabal working together to control the nation.*" It includes government organizations collecting private information, including phone call records, e-mails, text messages, also monitoring internet blogs, videos, and websites.

For many years, those researching globalism or the deep state have discovered eight different movements or organizations whose members and supporters are a close-knit cabal. Each group attempts to maintain secrecy related to their meetings, agendas, and strategies. These eight groups are:

- The New World Order Cabal
- The Global Government Cabal
- The Illuminati

- The Tri-Lateral Commission
- The Council on Foreign Relations
- The Bilderbergers
- The Bohemian Grove
- The Committee of 300

It would require a very lengthy book or documentary to explain the history and goals of each of the above-mentioned organizations. When any journalist, author, or film producer begins exposing the secrets of any of these groups, secularists and globalists immediately criticize their research as fabricated conspiracies. However, look at the different quotes from world leaders, including politicians who recognized the existence of such groups:

> *"It is not my intent to doubt that the Doctrines of the Illuminati, the principles of Jacobinism had not spread to the United States. On the contrary, no one is more truly satisfied of this fact than I am."*
>
> – George Washington

> *"Behind the ostensible government sits enthroned an invisible government owing no allegiance and acknowledging no responsibility to the people."*
>
> – Theodore Roosevelt

> *"It is the system of nationalist individualism that has to go...We are living in the end of sovereign states...In the great struggle to evoke a Westernized World Socialism, contemporary governments may vanish ...Countless people...will hate the New World Order...and will die protesting it."*
>
> – H.G. Wells in his 1940 book, The New World Order

"We shall have a world government, whether or not we like it. The question is only whether world government will be achieved by consent or conquest."

– James Warburg – His father was the head of the Federal Reserve

"The drive of the Rockefellers and their allies is to create a one-world government combining super-Capitalism and Communism under the same tent, all under their control...Do I mean conspiracy? Yes, I do. I am convinced there is such a plot, international in scope, generations old in planning, and incredibly evil in intent."

– Larry MacDonald – Democratic Senator, US House, Georgia

When the United States received independence from Great Britain, our young nation of thirteen colonies was a new global experiment. The Great Seal of the United States, first used in 1782, appears on the back of the dollar bill. Scrolled underneath the pyramid are the Latin words Novus Ordo Seclorum, meaning *New Order of the Ages.* After 245 years of American expansion and domination, a global reset society is determined to create another New World Order, this time by uniting nations. This required degrading America's Constitution, claiming it is now outdated and needs to be replaced. By condemning and mocking patriotism, dishonoring the elderly, and silencing America's conservative voices, the old order will diminish, and the new order will replace the void.

300 WEALTHY FAMILIES

There are approximately 300 extremely wealthy families scattered throughout the world's 195 nations. These families have either inherited their wealth, marketed personal inventions, or invested, multiplying their prosperity and affluence. They own gold, silver, copper, and gems mines. Others control the global oil and gas supplies, manipulating prices and some own massive swatches of land where food is produced. Some dominate global shipping and air transportation. These families are the CEOs of corporations and world banking. They have secured their wealth by expanding global investments, controlling trade, and controlling the distribution of goods.

Sometime back, I met a businessman whose family was originally from India. I became familiar with him, being in the same facility as him for two weeks. His father owned ships that hauled shipping containers around the world from ports in China. His family had profited billions of dollars in a single year. This man was dealing with stress, and I could see the cares of a global business on his face. For us average folks, we cannot comprehend dealing with that level of income.

These 300 families (combined) have trillions of dollars in wealth, office complexes, and personal assets. Their income and "connections" provide their children with the highest academic education in Ivy League Universities. These include Harvard, Yale, Princeton, Oxford, and Dartmouth.

When attending these universities, the young adults from these families meet other students from every nation, who are from privileged, wealthy families, including political families from the United States. Their family members control the secular media, newspapers, magazines, education, and transportation, along with major corporations such as Google, Apple, Amazon, Facebook, and so forth. While they differ in religion, culture, and social ideology, they all unite over wealth accumulation and being global influencers. At the university level, lifetime connections are made, enabling economic and political backscratching for generations. Many of these students graduate, later rising to leadership levels overseeing and developing new technologies.

Those in the computer and iPhone fields, without their knowledge, are often developing the technology that will be a part of the Antichrist and his "beast" kingdom for tracking, buying, and selling, using a mark and a number system.

THE SHADOW GOVERNMENT

For many years, students of prophecy have heard of a "shadow government," working behind the scenes, pulling economic strings, plotting the rise and fall of world leaders, also controlling large international financial loans and interest rates. A good definition of a shadow government is, *"When political power does not reside in our elected representatives but in private individuals who control them."* The bait these economic kingpins use to hook politicians is large corporative donations providing a political candidate with tools for self-promotion, getting them elected to a seat in the legislative branch, ensuring that as their political puppet passes laws, the financial favor will be returned in legislation favoring the corporation. I am familiar with several very wealthy business entrepreneurs. When they support politicians, they often donate to both Democrats and Republicans to ensure they have the favor of both sides.

Years ago, when men were lining up in the presidential primaries, I was invited to meet with a billionaire who asked my two politically-connected friends and me to make contact with a Senator from a southern state who was one of the possible presidential candidates. Our intent for this invitation was to invite this Senator to speak in our town. However, I found out that the businessman was having difficulty in this Senator's state involving legal action being taken against him and his large businesses there. After hearing the Senator may come to our town, the man wanted to meet the Senator to see if he would assist him with this matter. This was not our intention or purpose, and we left his office, choosing to cancel the invitation.

INVITATION TO THE BILDERBERGERS

Through close friends, I have become familiar with how this shadow government works. I have a close Jewish friend from Israel who became a Messianic believer. His father was a high-level Israeli official, working undercover for Israeli intelligence, traveling for special assignments for many years. When his father died, Israeli intelligence services came to his father's house in black vans, sweeping through the entire home, collecting papers and barrels of materials. Because my friend's father had global connections with world leaders, when the Bilderbergers met in Jerusalem, he was invited to their private meetings.

During this meeting in Jerusalem, which was many years ago, the group spoke of banking and the coming financial crisis, noting problems in Greece, Spain, Jerusalem, and the United States. They discussed how they could benefit from these economic challenges and how the banking and interest rates could be manipulated in the major banks of Europe and the United States, including the International Monetary Fund. These men were part of the "shadow men" that manipulate events in nations, oversee international loans, set lending interest rates, even manipulating the collapse and reformation of nations and their leaders.

As a result of his "connections," he told me of a strange incident that was quite interesting. He was visited by a man who was close to his father and also knew him. He worked for the U.S. government and carried a special computer. This man had all the private phone numbers of noted people, including ministers, and could monitor their phone records. He asked him, "Do you want to talk to so-and-so," naming a well-known minister that I will not identify. My friend had met this famous minister once. The government official called a private cell-phone number. The minster answered, asking my friend who had given him this private number? He asked, "How did you get this number. No one has this number, not even my family." My friend never told him it was a government agent who had his private number. The conversation was brief.

My friend then asked, "Why do you have these numbers, and how can you even listen in on the calls?" His answer was, "We find out if they are doing anything that could get them in trouble or be used against them later. For example, if a minister preached something we don't like or attacks a certain government publicly, we can release information we have *to certain people in the media* through a third party and shut them up by exposing them or changing the public's perception of them."

WORSHIPPERS OF LUCIFER

Years ago, when Obama was President, my friend, Bishop Dennis McGuire, asked if I would meet with several men from an Eastern European nation. One was a wealthy businessman who requested to meet personally with me. They had watched me on television, in their European nation, and for some reason felt I was "famous" and could contact President Obama on their behalf. The businessman had a large factory located in Germany. A former Communist country owed him 700 million dollars for constructing their transit system. He had become a Christian.

Due to his European business, connections, and wealth, he was privy to dine and speak personally with the inner-circle leadership of many European governments. Speaking through an interpreter, he began explaining how many leaders in Europe were raised Catholic or Orthodox, but their love for power and money turned them from their Christian upbringing, and many were now Luciferins. I had never heard this term and asked for an explanation. He replied:

> *"In the Bible, Satan offered Jesus the kingdoms of this world, and He rejected them. Paul also wrote that Satan was the god of this world and prince of the power of the air. The Luciferin groups don't see Satan as an evil fallen angel, but one who is equal with God. To them, God rules heaven, but Satan rules the earth. For them, if Satan offered Jesus the kingdoms of this world, they believe by praying to and serving Satan as another god, he will grant them favor, wealth, and power to rule the world."*

He then informed me that on several occasions, he was invited to small, private dinners with leaders of nations, where the head was calling for Lucifer's favor and blessings to be with them.

I later researched Luciferianism on the internet, where it confirmed the information. The articles revealed that Luciferins support the protection of the natural world and are focused on this life. The main goals are enlightenment and worship of the inner self. This worship of Lucifer began in Medieval times. According to this first-hand eyewitness, there is a secretive group still practicing this form of occultism.

POWER TO THE BEAST

The energy and global influence of the future Antichrist to control the world is directly given to him by Satan himself. John revealed this in Revelation, saying:

> *"And the beast which I saw was like unto a leopard, and his feet were as the feet of a bear, and his mouth as the mouth of a lion: and the dragon gave him his power, and his seat, and great authority"*
>
> – REVELATION 13:2

The Greek word here for *power* is *dunamis*, a word referring to the power to do miracles. The word *dragon* in Greek is the word for *serpent*. A serpent is a biblical symbol for Satan, a fallen angel who will give a specific area of rule and authority to the Antichrist. The Greek word here for *crown* refers to a *diadem*, which in Greek is a ruler's crown. The final world government will actually be under the direct control of Satan.

THE LOVE OF MONEY

It is not money in itself but the "love of money" that is the root of all evil. When the threat of Climate Change became a national crisis, the families of noted politicians began investing their money in "new green technology," including solar panels, wind turbines, and electric cars, as informed investors invest where future money is to be made. When COVID hit, there were already certain pharmaceuticals that were used to treat the virus, including one I took that helped me within 48 hours. However, these pills have been available for many years to help prevent malaria but were ignored or not permitted to be sold, as the companies creating the vaccines and various doctors put the word out that these pills were not effective, and only the vaccine would work. According to whistleblower-doctors, the underlying reason for rejecting a cheaper pill is because vaccines would create more money.

Each year, federal government agencies are budgeted a certain amount of money to spend. If within twelve months, any money is left over, the money allotted the following year is cut. To ensure their money is spent, departments have "meetings" in resorts such as Los Vegas, enjoying expensive hotels and meals to spend what remains, ensuring to not lose money for the following year. Investigations have shown this is one reason money spent on government contractors is often higher — the more spent — the more "needed" the following year.

In the past, if a government agency saved any money, that amount is deducted from the next year's budget. To prevent a Pentagon budget from being cut, it is always helpful to be in a war or have troops scattered throughout the world.

THE LUST FOR POWER

When Christ was tested by Satan in the wilderness for forty days, one of the concluding three temptations was for Christ to become a world ruler. We read:

> *"And the devil, taking him up into a high mountain, shewed unto him all the kingdoms of the world in a moment of time. And the devil said unto him, All this power will I give thee, and the glory of them: for that is delivered unto me; and to whomsoever I will I give it."*
>
> – Luke 4:5-6

The adversary spoke of *power*, which in Greek refers to *delegated authority*. Satan then mentioned *glory*. In Greek, *glory* can also refer to *honor*. Satan was making an appeal to Christ's pride, saying, "I will ensure that you have great authority and will be honored by people in the world if you just bow to me." How can Satan tempt the very one who was with God when the world was formed? Christ refused the offer.

Why do most Washington politicians have such a drive to remain in power? I am certain that some sincerely desire to make a positive contribution to the nation. However, it seems the longer they remain in a position of authority, it becomes about the money, fame, and power which becomes their dope, their cocaine driving them. They yielded to the temptation Christ rejected to receive the "authority and honor" of the people. Be grateful if your elected officials are honest, sincere, and making a positive impact.

INFORMATION COLLECTING

The Deep State is a surveillance state. China is the surveillance capital of the world. Their citizens are monitored and traced with cameras using facial recognition as well as through their iPhones. Collecting and monitoring personal information in the United States includes data from your laptop camera and microphone. If you can see and speak to another person using an iPhone, then high-tech equipment can see, hear, and record you. Although denied, Siri can listen in not only when you say, "Hey Siri," but as long as the small box is turned on. The camera and microphone on your home computer can be remotely accessed. Even certain types of alarm systems and certain infant security cameras can be hacked, enabling a person to see into your home. It is interesting that the CEOs of computer companies often place dark tape over their camera and microphone.

Anytime you access the internet, by phone or computer, there are companies using special programs to capture your information. They monitor the websites you visit, the information you have posted, advertisements you have viewed, and store the information on massive mainframes, collecting data on your browsing history. This information collection includes buying habits, places you've purchased coffee, and restaurants you have visited. Years ago, one large Social Media site hired four hundred people to sit at computers and look at the pictures people were posting.

On several occasions, I have met and spoken to retired men that once worked inside government facilities whose job was "tracking and storing" data. In every case, the higher they were, the more apt they were (upon retiring) to have no electronics such as iPhones, laptops, or smart televisions. They communicated the old school way, on a landline. Most were living in the country, far from cities where they grew their own food, drilled wells, raise cattle and chickens. At times, they will use special equipment and do "sweeps" of each room in their house or office to detect electronic listening devices. They are not hyper, but they are knowledgeable.

MY FRIEND

To protect my friend, I will not use his real name or his location. Years ago, he and his entire family lived near a military base in Maryland. This base was used by the U.S. government to research and develop biological weapons in special labs. Over time, various chemicals and dangerous substances were placed in metal barrels, sealed, and buried underground in a field near the facilities. After several years, large numbers of people (1,800 of them) living in a large nearby town were diagnosed with cancer. His own young daughter and wife, both who had lived in the town, died with cancer.

With the death of his daughter, he began researching the experiments with bio-weapons at the military base. Several whistleblowers came forward informing him that they believed the town's water supply was contaminated and compromised by leaking metal barrels. My friend forced the base to conduct a public hearing in which he presented clear evidence of what was occurring, proving the source of the cancer was a result of the military base's failure to properly secure the chemicals. Because of two family deaths and the suffering in the local town, he brought a major lawsuit against the base and the government, hoping to use any income from the suit to help those suffering.

A VISIT AND A THREAT

After the lawsuit was announced publicly, he was eating at a restaurant in the south when two men in black suits entered the facility, walked to his table, and sat down — uninvited. They informed him they were special ops from the base in Maryland. They warned him that he should drop the lawsuit and be quiet, or it may "cost him" down the road. He told them he was not afraid of them, as he knew what it was to experience loss throughout his life. One then pulled out a small, sealed glass vial of liquid. The man warned, "Just a few drops of this in your food, and you will be dead." They stood up and walked out.

A few weeks later, he became deathly sick. He and his church prayed, not knowing what he was dealing with. I told him to get to a local center for disease control, or a hospital, and tell them that he believes he was poisoned. After a blood test, they discovered four types of dangerous metals and chemicals in his body, one of which should have killed him. Eventually, his lawyers determined that two of the dangerous chemicals may have been sent through his home air-vents. A short time later, he found his dog dead—by poison. A few weeks later, while driving, the tires on his cars blew out. When he had them replaced, the shop manager said, "Someone cut just enough on the inside not to flatten them. However, when you sped up on the road, the pressure blew them out." It was a professional job. He also told me that he has documented evidence of over 16 scientists, all of whom are now dead, that worked at the lab. It was also a lab where scientists worked on viruses. It is believed to be the same lab that anthrax originated from shortly after 9-11.

SPYING ON HIM

There were times he was sitting in his house, forming a legal strategy, only to discover that the government lawyers had pre-empted it. This happened over and over again. His plans were to try the case at the Supreme Court. However, again and again, the process was blocked.

Because of a loss of income, he moved out of his house. Someone had *given* him a giant painting of Christ in a huge and heavy gold, wooden frame. The picture had been hanging on his wall in an open area. When the heavy painting was lifted from off the wall, it slipped, falling to the ground, breaking one of the frame's wooden edges. When it broke, he saw wires and a small hidden camera concealed in the lower corner! He realized that he was being spied on the entire time. The camera was checked by a specialist. It was clear this hidden camera was concealed by a professional.

This is the very reason why people back off from challenging the government, especially on a federal level. One individual who was a former government employee with top-secret clearance made the statement, "That poor man will end up dead before they ever give him one penny." He has turned all the documents over to legal firms in the event of his death.

THE COVER-UPS

By now, most discerning conservative Americans know that anyone who is a part of the Deep-State Cabal receives the protection of the men and women within their inner-circle. A prime example is Hillary Clinton. Much of what she did with her personal servers and e-mails broke federal laws. She placed a personal server in her closet that held several classified e-mails that, by law, were only to be on a government-protected classified server. She then erased tens of thousands of e-mails to prevent them from being downloaded by investigators. She had her computer hard drive wiped clean to prevent professionals from finding what she had written, and she destroyed phones. She broke election laws by contacting a foreign government and paying for fake information to trap Trump. There are also questionable donations for the Clinton Foundation from world leaders to perhaps gain political favors. Despite all of this, why was she protected and never charged for criminal misconduct?

The answers seem to be clear from released e-mails and texts. The leading officers in the F.B.I., C.I.A., and N.S.A., along with most workers in the Federal Government, not only believed she would be elected president in 2016 but were *preparing* Washington for her to be president. According to inside sources, she was already placing an order for curtains in the White House the day of the election. Also, she was head of the Justice Department, a position giving her access to anyone's private files. As one former federal worker suggested, "She likely had access to all of the "dirt" on everyone in high-level positions, and they were basically afraid of her retaliating against them. She could leak personal secrets to her media friends, eventually destroying someone's reputation.

Her decades of working inside the government (state and federal) provided countless opportunities to meet and link with thousands of other government politicians and agency directors, providing her an edge during numerous controversies. In a normal local community, friendships are forged lasting a lifetime. Close friends defend close friends. The same is true in politics.

SOME BASIC ADVICE

Most Americans are concerned about three things:

1. We wish to live in a nation that provides the freedom to publicly speak, write opinions, and worship God without fear of retaliation.

2. We wish to secure a good job with fair wages to build wealth and provide for our families.

3. We wish to have the right to own property, a home, have the freedom to buy and sell, to protect and defend our property, home, possession, and families.

All believers must keep in mind that we are "in this world but not of the world." Paul wrote that a great shaking would come to the earth. However, we are part of God's kingdom which cannot be shaken. Our freedoms are God-given and not political weapons to be used by political opponents.

CHAPTER 14

AMERICA: WHERE ANCIENT EMPIRES MEET

America has been called "The Melting Pot." This phrase was first used in the 1780s. It is a metaphor describing the blending of nationalities, cultures, races, and religions in America. When immigrants arrive from other nations, they are immigrants until they apply for and receive American citizenship. After a swearing-in ceremony, they become "official" Americans. It is likely that people from all 195 nations on earth live somewhere in America. With all of our immigrants, we are also home to the descendants of the ancient empires that once ruled from the Middle East, Europe, and around the Mediterranean Sea.

From a biblical perspective, beginning with Babylon until the eighth and final kingdom, prophetic history identifies the below empires, ending with the final Empire of the Antichrist:

THE EMPIRE	THE DATE OF RULE	THE AREA OF THE WORLD
Babylonian	606 BC – 561 BC	Iraq, Syria, Lebanon, Armenia, Israel
Media/Persian	538 BC – 330 BC	Iraq, Iran, Syria, Lebanon, Egypt, Afghanistan

Grecian Empire	330 BC – 146 BC	Iraq, Iran, Greece, North Africa, Turkey to India
Roman Empire	146 BC – AD 476	Around the entire Mediterranean Sea area (west)
The Seventh Empire	A Future Empire	Began with the Turkish Empire, leading to the E.U.
The Future 10 Kings	The Final Empire	Forming a future final kingdom of 10 kings

Daniel chapter ten presents a stunning revelation explaining how strong, demonic spirits are given a command-center over nations, especially those whose military and economic decisions impact Israel, Jerusalem, and the Jewish people. This invisible cosmic struggle is very real. God Himself assigned the highest-ranking archangel, Michael, as the guardian and sole protector of the nation of Israel (Dan. 10:21;12:1). The Old and New Testaments clearly express that Michael is the only angel afforded direct authority from God to battle one-on-one with (fallen angel) Satan (Jude 9; Rev. 12:7-10).

Each biblical empire had its own type of government, its own religion (a mix of false gods and goddesses), its own traditions, customs, and forums. Secular historians pour over every type of historical document, helping compile an exhaustive study that details each empire. However, what is seldom taught are the types of spirits, including demonic chief spirits that dominated the upper atmosphere, overseeing specific activities in that particular empire.

ANCIENT SPIRITS OVER AMERICA

Having researched for several decades, I have learned how those ancient spirits have gained access to America. After all, ancient, angelic, and demonic spirits never die. They simply transition to new empires.

Looking at the back of a one-dollar-bill, the Great Seal of the United States includes a pyramid with a missing capstone. The Pyramids are a huge part of Egyptian history. The American idea behind using the pyramid was the concept of America lasting as long as the pyramids have, for thousands of years. The pyramid is unfinished, indicating the work of America would always continue. On the National Mall in Washington D.C. stands a 555-foot-high obelisk, another early symbol originating in Egypt, called the Washington Monument. It was once the tallest structure in the world, between 1884-1989. American designers often used early Egyptian symbolism.

The early biblical reference for Egypt is found in Genesis and Exodus. This empire, back in the time of Moses, was oppressing the Hebrew people that were living among them, forcing them into slavery. They worked continually to build massive treasure cities for Pharaoh. The *spirit* of Egypt is a mix of idolatry and slavery. The goal of this spirit is to bring a free people under complete control of the government and its leaders.

In biblical order, the Assyrian Empire followed the Egyptians. The Assyrians were responsible for a major separation among Israel's tribes. The kingdom of Israel split into the Northern and Southern Kingdoms. In 722 BC, Israel's northern headquarters, Samaria, was seized by the Assyrian king and his army. The ten northern tribes were deported out of the country, eventually scattered among the Gentile nations. They became "the lost ten tribes." When historians write about Assyrian history, their leadership in taking tens of thousands of Jews into captivity will forever remain a stain on their empire's resumé, in the same manner of the Jewish Holocaust and Germany. The spirit of Assyria is one that stirs up division within the nation.

Another empire that negatively impacted Jerusalem and the Jews was the Empire of Babylon, led by King Nebuchadnezzar. The Babylonian government administrated strict laws, including control over the types of food consumed (Dan. 1), how and when to worship (Dan. 6), including punishing those who refused to bow to idols. Historically, Babylon (and the surrounding region) was steeped in all forms of idolatry, including temple worship to the sun, moon, and stars, making it an oppressive land for any righteous person to live in. The Jews in Babylon became so despondent, they sat by the river, hanging their harps on the willow trees, refusing to sing a song to the Lord in this strange land (Psa. 137:1-3). Babylon is the spirit that counters true worship.

After seventy years, the neighboring Medes and Persians diverted the Euphrates river into trenches, invading Babylon by night, entering the city, and overthrowing the Babylonian King. While the lords and princes feasted in a massive banquet hall, God took His finger and wrote a warning on the wall that time had run out for the Babylonian Empire.

The Persians were known for passing laws that could not be broken. The two political-military leaders, Darius and Cyrus, were friendly to the Jews, permitting the Jewish captives in Babylon to pack up and return to Jerusalem. However, there were political opponents in the kingdom, who were jealous of Daniel, enforcing new laws against prayer, hoping to trap the elder Hebrew prophet, sending him to his death. The spirit of Persia includes the spirit that passes laws to prevent religious freedom or religious expression.

Eventually, a new empire ruled the known world under the leadership of Alexander the Great. The Greeks were a proud people who prided themselves on wisdom, philosophy, knowledge, and intellect.

The term *philosophy* means "love of wisdom." The ultimate goal of a Greek male was to achieve wisdom and illumination concerning the cosmos, nature, and human life. The list of Greek philosophers includes Aristotle, Epicurus, Democritus, Plato, Socrates, and numerous others.

There is carnal and spiritual wisdom. Seeking wisdom without the scripture, you will fall short of truth and have few answers to complexities in life. You will never understand why you were created or your divine purpose. The spirit of the ancient Greeks is rooted in *humanism.* The humanist emphasizes you, the power in you, your ability, and that you are a little god. Humanism theorized we are all good in some way, and we can tap into deep rational thinking to solve life's problems. Humanism is the spirit behind many institutions of higher learning.

Without question, the spirit of the Roman Empire was one of *tolerance*, as Roman authorities were tolerant as long as you followed all of the rules and regulations laid down by Rome. Breaking the law meant immediate conflict with soldiers, governors, and judges. Offenders were sent to prison, awaiting a trial, and if found guilty, punishment or execution. The spirit of Rome is one that seemed to be patient with different religions, except one that stirred up the people or may threaten a massive following, leading to a rebellion.

My point is that these *spirits* that assisted world leaders in the ancient empires of prophecy did not die when the empires faded, becoming a chapter in the world history books. The angel Gabriel revealed to Daniel the names of two of the highest-level prince spirits ruling the upper atmosphere in Babylon: the prince of Persia and the prince of Grecia (Dan. 10). Since America is a melting pot of nations, we are also a cauldron mixed with every form of religious beliefs and opinions.

With a new global-Babel/Babylonian style reset, those living in the United States will be dealing with men and women in high positions who will, without their knowledge, be yielding to the same spirits that motivated the kings and leaders from the dynasties of Egypt to Imperial Rome. There will be laws passed contrary to the scriptures, intolerance toward religious freedom, and a spirit of division and bondage that leads many to become depressed and oppressed.

We must become Daniels in Babylon. He prayed three times a day, used his spiritual gifts to plan for the future, never compromised his faith, and remained true, under persecution, to what he believed. His companions took the attitude, live or die, we will not bow to idols or a system that is opposite of God's higher laws. Remember, we will all answer to God in the end, not to man.

CHAPTER 15

HAS AMERICA ENTERED HER FULLNESS OF TIME?

Time can be measured in years, months, weeks, days, hours, minutes, and seconds. Biblical prophecy is when holy men visualizes events in the future, often centuries or thousands of years before it happens. When the set time comes for a prophet's words to be fulfilled, that moment is called "the fullness of time" (Eph. 1:10). For example, let's look at Christ's birth. From the time of Adam when the Father tells the serpent that the seed of the woman would crush his head to the birth of Christ, it is believed that a timeframe of approximately 4,000 years passes. Paul gave a unique insight into Christ's birth when he wrote:

> *"But when the fullness of the time had come, God sent forth His Son, born of a woman, born under the law, to redeem those who were under the law, that we might receive the adoption as sons."*
>
> – Galatians 4:4-5 (NKJV)

The key phrase is "fullness of time." The Greek word fullness is *pleroma*, referring to something that becomes *complete or full, such as filling a container.* In this context, it is connected with time. If you plan to have a lunch meeting at noon (when you wake up in the morning at six), then nine o'clock, ten o'clock, and eleven o'clock is not the fullness of time. Only at noon does the set time arrive.

Why did the Heavenly Father wait for four millenniums before sending His Son, the Messiah? The answer can be found when understanding the impact of the Greek culture, the Roman Empire, and the occupation of Roman soldiers in Judea and Jerusalem.

Christ would make disciples, form a new living fellowship called the church, introduce a new kingdom, the kingdom of God, and transfer His spiritual authority to His followers, giving them the ability to expel spirits and heal the suffering. The time was "ripe" for a new covenant of redemption.

THE FIVE ELEMENTS NEEDED

Before Christ could come to earth, there had to be 5 things in place: road transportation, ships, established languages, coinage, and gathering places for worship. Christ and His disciples needed these things in order to bring the Gospel and the evangelistic message throughout the Roman Empire and beyond. The Romans created thousands of roads for travel and transporting goods on horseback, donkeys, and carts. The Greeks were master *shipbuilders*, carrying people and goods to shipping ports built along the coastal cities of the Mediterranean Sea. The inscription on the cross reveals there were three main *languages* spoken at the time of Christ in and around Israel: Roman citizens spoke Latin, Gentile nations spoke Greek, and Jews spoke Hebrew in Jerusalem and Judea. There were several types of coinage used: Greek, Roman, and Jewish. The Romans minted bronze, silver, and gold coins that were used throughout the empire. There were synagogues, theatres, and amphitheaters used to accommodate religious worshippers and city-wide events.

All of this had to be in place at the time of Christ's birth and at the formation of the Christian Church. Paul was converted on a Roman road that connected Israel to Damascus called "The road to Damascus." The city of Rome had 29 major military roads leading in and out of the city in all directions. Late in Rome's 113 provinces, 372 roads connected the empire. The roads covered 250,000 miles, with 20 percent being paved with stones.[1] Roman and Greek cities (including those Paul addressed in his epistles and John wrote to in the Apocalypse) could all be accessed by anyone walking, riding on horseback or donkeys, or by driving chariots or wooden carts. The roads were the connections to the cities. By the year AD 256, Rome operated 330 ships. These were used in the Navy and to transport grains and all types of traded goods.[2] In Acts, Paul often traveled the seas on a ship, evangelizing new cities during his missionary journeys (Acts 21:2-6; 27:2-44; 28:11). The New Testament's 27 books were written in the Koine (common) Greek language, a language that was spoken in practically every nation. This enabled the New Testament letters to be related to believers by someone reading the Greek text, then translating the words for hearers of a different language. Outside of Jerusalem, the two main languages were Greek and Latin. The more educated Romans also read and spoke Greek. The coinage minted by Rome was accepted in Asia and Northern Africa. Thus, if an offering was received in Judea, it could be taken to Asia to assist the church. This was true in every city. The timing of the construction of the large, Greek-Roman theatres that provided opportunities for a general assembly of the city must also be pointed out. In these outdoor settings, the Apostles drew multitudes to debate the Scriptures, testifying of their personal conversion, or gathering a crowd to proclaim the death, burial, and resurrection of Christ (Acts 19:29). All of these components, the roads, ships, common language, main currency, and facilities to host crowds, were important and necessary devices to help spread the message of Christ and to expand and connect the Christian community, helping advance the kingdom and provide finances.

AMERICA'S SOVEREIGN ROLE

Without drawing out the long history of America, our nation was raised up by the Divine providence of the Almighty for numerous national and global purposes. At the conclusion of World War II, the influence of the British Empire began to weaken as America began surpassing Britain and England in technology, economic growth, and military prowess when she introduced the nuclear age. The dollar became the global reserve currency, causing the New York Stock Exchange and New York City to become the global center for economic activity, whose trading and selling of stocks impacted all world markets. In the United States, major Christian television networks were born to carry the Gospel by satellite throughout the world. For several decades, Christians in America have financed countless world mission outreaches, Bible schools, orphanages, digging fresh water wells, printing and distributing Bibles in every language. Since my call into ministry in the late 1970s, I have seen diverse ministries fill large auditoriums, megachurches, and conference centers with thousands in attendance, all hearing life-changing messages of faith.

The appearance of Christ happened when time was "full" or complete, and global events were in proper alignment. Israel's unbelief opened the door for the Gentiles to receive the New Covenant. The spiritual blindness and rejection of the Gospel in America will again open the door for "All of Israel to be saved" (Rom. 11:26). With Israel's blindness, Gentiles were grafted into the covenant. When the Gentiles go spiritually blind, Israel's salvation begins.

DEATH TO THE RIGHTEOUS—A SIGN

The book of Genesis records ten generations of men from Adam to Noah. In the six hundredth year of Noah's life, the flood arrived. Prior to that day, all righteous men had died, with the exception of Noah, who was "perfect and upright in his generation" (Gen. 6:9). God was patient to wait until all of the righteous men were taken by death, then within a short time, the floodwaters exploded on the earth.

The book of Jasher, a non-canonical book that is mentioned in Joshua 10:13 and 2 Samuel 1:18, lists the names of Jacob's twelve sons, including the number of years they lived in Egypt until their deaths. The Pharaoh to whom Joseph served as second in command, and Joseph's large family of Hebrews worked well together until the death of the last Hebrew patriarch. According to Jasher, when Jacob's last son died, the new Pharaoh did not know the amazing historical link between Joseph saving Egypt and the king of Egypt's favor showed to Joseph's family. Shortly after the last patriarch's death, the new king brought the Hebrews under the servitude of Egypt, leading to captivity and slavery.

In America, something similar is occurring. In the early 1990s, there were over 20 different ministers preaching at the yearly International Prophecy Conference in Tampa, Florida. Presently, over 85% of these men are now in heaven. This list identifies the prophetic teachers who are now with the Lord:

- Ray Brubaker
- Dr. Jack Van Impe
- Tim Lahaye
- Chuck Smith
- Chuck Missler

- David Allen Lewis
- Dr. Dave Breeze
- Yacov Rambsel
- Grant Jefferies
- J.R. Church
- Zola Levitt
- Irvine Baxter
- Dave Hunt
- David Wilkerson

Only a few older men, now living, continue sounding the warning trumpet, "prepare for the return of the Lord." In a strange twist, prophetic teacher, Irvine Baxter, passed away on the same day, according to the Jewish calendar, that the flood of Noah began. This was also close to the time of the 2020 United States Presidential election. On that day, thousands of years ago, a violent flood of destruction overtook the earth, shaking the entire planet, literally changing the natural form of the earth, ushering in a new global reset.

POST-FLOOD EVENTS

The rain continued pounding the earth for forty days and nights. However, even when the rain stopped, Noah had to remain in confinement (lockdown) for 150 days, or five straight months. It was slightly over one year from the day the flood began that Noah and his family exited the Ark and began the long process of forming a new world order.

Prophetic ministers use the signs in Genesis 6 to prove we are in the time of the end. In my research, I noticed the signs in Noah's day continued past the flood to the forming a new government order. The new reforming of the earth led to a city called Babel, organized by a strong leader-dictator named Nimrod (Gen 11).

The COVID virus is one of the five global pandemics that have impacted the earth over a period of time. History records there was the plague in Athens in 430 BC that lasted for five years with a death toll of 100,000 people. The Antoine Plague in AD 165-180, carried by Roman soldiers, destroyed the army and may have killed up to 5 million people. During the plague of Cyprian in AD 250-271, the bishop said the epidemic was the "end of the world." It was killing about 5,000 people a day in Rome, requiring the dead to be burned in kilns. In modern times, the Spanish Flu was the world's most deadly plague until COVID arrived. The COVID death numbers have not risen to the level of the Spanish Flu (at this point), but COVID effectively shut down the entire world's economy, especially travel.

Two events unfolded after Noah left the Ark. The first was when Noah got drunk and laid naked in his tent after planting a vineyard, harvesting the grapes, and making wine (Gen. 9:20-21). In the New Testament, Christ warned to beware of becoming careless prior to His return, including a stern warning against drunkenness (Luke 21:34). Noah was so drunk that he exposed himself, and some believe that while he was in a drunken stupor, his grandson (referred to as son in KJV), Canaan took advantage of the old man in a carnal way. The two sons of Noah Shem and Japeth realized this and, walking backward, covered their dad with a large blanket. However, we read, "When Noah awoke from his wine, and knew what his younger son had done, he said, cursed be Canaan" (Gen. 9:24-25). According to some, this particular act is comparable to the same type of immoral activity that is now commonly accepted. In the post-flood era, God also gave a warning on shedding innocent blood. We read, "Whoever sheds man's blood, by man shall his blood be shed" (Gen. 9:6). America and other Gentile nations legally abort infants. In the United States, the aborted organs are stored in refrigerators, later to be sold for research. Another post-flood change was God's promise not to destroy the world again with water, conformed when He set His bow, a rainbow, in the sky as a visible sign of a covenant to prevent a future global judgment by water. In our time, the gay community has taken the rainbow as its symbol.

THE FULLNESS OF AMERICA

Has America arrived at the climax of her assignment as a Judeo-Christian-based Empire? An army of new progressives is positioned in high levels of authority at local, state, and federal government levels. They scream for tolerance but have no tolerance for strong Bible-believing Christians, patriots, or those whose ideas are founded on spiritual, moral, or fiscal conservative beliefs. America has been the leading Gentile nation in five areas:

- Military capabilities
- Controlling and determining the world's economic stability
- Assisting nations in natural disaster relief
- Supporting the poor, the needy, the orphans, and disenfranchised
- Preaching, teaching, and declaring the Gospel of Jesus Christ

America has experienced awakenings, revivals, and outpourings of the Spirit for hundreds of years. Between 1700 and 1740, nearly eighty percent of those living in the colonies attended church. From the mid-1700s through the 1800s, churches were built in cities and in rural areas. The majority of the population attended church regularly each Sunday morning.[3] However, by the twentieth century, with Darwinism, Evolution, Atheism, Humanism, and other -isms in colleges and universities, the religious fever began declining. Today in America, only 25% percent of the population attends church once a week. While 25% seldom do and 29% never do.[4] Statistics indicate that Americans are moving away from their faith, including church attendance, as they feel it is irrelevant to our modern culture. They are becoming dull of hearing and blind in their spiritual vision.

Paul presented a powerful discourse about the effects of spiritual blindness in Romans chapter 11. This epistle was written by Paul to the Gentile churches meeting in Rome. The eleventh chapter of Romans explains this "fullness" concept. Paul uses the metaphor of two olive trees: one natural, which is Israel, the other a wild olive tree, which represents the Gentiles. He noted that Israel was presented the Gospel first, but the nation as a whole fell into unbelief. Thus, some branches on the tree of Israel were severed, providing the opportunity for God to graft in wild branches from the Gentile tree. This interpretation is that the Gentiles would be grafted into the New Covenant (Rom. 11:17-20).

Paul noted that Israel's spiritual blindness opened the door of opportunity for the eyes of the Gentiles to be opened. As long as the Gentiles would receive the Gospel and believe in Christ, they would bear spiritual fruit on their branches. However, the day would eventually come when Gentiles would begin rejecting the preaching of Christ, becoming spiritually blind and refusing to repent. Paul wrote, "Blindness in part has happened to Israel, until the fullness of the Gentiles comes in" (Rom. 11:25). Paul taught that if Israel would remove their unbelief, God could graft them back into the covenant tree (Rom. 11:23).

Paul warned the Gentiles that they should avoid pride, arrogance, and unbelief. New statistics reveal there is a shortage of strong spiritual faith in America, including a decline in following moral laws and spiritual principles (from the scriptures) that made this nation great.

The fullness of America is when:

1. God's sovereign purpose for the nation has been completed
2. The inhabitants of the land reject the Bible and its principles
3. The people in the nation no longer repent and harden their hearts toward truth
4. Abominations are made legal and acceptable to the majority of the people

When these four actions unite at the same time, the fullness of time has arrived.

The fullness factor does not indicate America will be destroyed, cease to exist, or become a non-entity. When national sins, unbelief, and rejection of God's laws persist, according to the patters in ancient Israel, the following will occur:

1. God will permit the nation to be surrounded by bad leaders
2. God will permit strangers to rise up higher than His own people
3. God will deliver us to the will of those who hate us
4. God will permit economic challenges
5. God will lift His hand, allowing natural disasters

The purpose of such distress is to lead men to repentance. Only the repentant man or woman can enter the eternal kingdom of God.

AMERICA'S FULLNESS OF TIME IN A NUTSHELL

Prophetically, when national sins overtake the majority in a nation's population, as it did in the days of Noah, the "cup of iniquity becomes full." This fullness of iniquity is often the trigger, releasing the "fullness of time," which, in historical terms, leads to the soon collapse of nations and empires. America, at this time, is presently fulfilling a series of parallel cycles, indicating, once again, that history does and will repeat itself. Here are some parallels:

- Parallels with the same political spirits controlling ancient Babel and Babylon
- Parallels with ancient Israel, with immoral and bad leaders rising and ruling
- Parallels with Imperial Rome, mirroring the type of division between east and west
- Parallels with Rome's cycle of emperors who strategized to limit and suppress religious freedom
- Parallels with the same sins that destroyed Sodom and Gomorrah
- Parallels with warnings to Jerusalem of shedding innocent blood and the judgment that followed
- Parallels with the same strategy Balaam used that self-cursed Israel
- Parallels with the clash between the attacks of Jezebel and the anointing of Elijah

These combined repetitive, cyclical patterns are visible evidence that we are living in the time of the end, the predicted set time alluded to by the visionary prophets of the ancient scripture. For those without a redemptive covenant, the future is dark, depressive, and bleak. However, for those who have experienced the new covenant of redemption through Christ, we have a secure future. Yet, part of our assignment is to be knowledgeable and teach others what is planned in the future and how to be spiritually and emotionally prepared. Hopefully, what you have read has presented important insights that will provoke your spirit and enlighten your understanding.

CLOSING

Words and phrases evolve over decades of time. The new secular phrase is "Global Reset." Without their knowledge, the globalists are preparing the way for what Daniel and the Apostle John identified as "The Kingdom of the Beast." Should the national leaders in the United States compromise our freedoms and merge with Europe in a new economic and social reset, we will eventually find ourselves in the early stages of John's Apocalyptic vision, identified as the book of Revelation.

It is no longer a matter of if this will happen. It's only a matter of when it will begin. Until that time comes, we must all tap into wisdom, knowledge, and understanding in planning, preparing, and most of all, praying for the Almighty to favor His remnant of true believers scattered throughout the nations. Always remember, as followers of Christ, we are a nation within a nation, a kingdom within a kingdom, a people with a future that has been designed and prepared from the foundation of the world. The real reset, called the millennial reign of the Messiah, is the one we will be directly involved in. Stay strong, fight the good fight, never quit or give up, and pray for wisdom in all of your future decisions. As Solomon once wrote, "Wisdom is better than strength," and "Wisdom is better than weapons of war" (Eccl. 9:16, 18).

NOTES

Introduction: Free Eagles and Cages Don't Get Along

1. The American Eagle Foundation
www.eagles.org
https://www.eagles.org/what-we-do/educate/learn-about-eagles/bald-eagle-usas-national-symbol/
(accessed January 30, 2021)

Chapter 1: Ancient Babel-Globalism Now Taking Effect

1. Wikipedia, The Free Encyclopedia
"Nimrod"
www.Wikepedia.org
https://en.wikipedia.org/wiki/Nimrod
(accessed January 30, 2021)

2. Flavius Josephus, The Antiquities of the Jews
Book 1, Chapter 4, Section 3
(accessed January 30, 2021)

3. Bank of England, KnowledgeBank
"What is an Exchange Rate?"
www.bankofengland.co.uk
https://www.bankofengland.co.uk/knowledgebank/who-sets-exchange-rates
(accessed January 30,2021)

4. Lexico, Powered by Oxford
www.lexico.com
https://www.lexico.com/en/definition/humanism
(accessed February 3, 2021)

5. NPR, WUTC 88.1 Chattanooga NPR Station
"How 5 Tech Giants Have Become More Like Governments Than Companies"
www.npr.org
https://www.npr.org/2017/10/26/560136311/how-5-tech-giants-have-become-more-like-governments-than-companies
(accessed February 3, 2021)

6. Business Insider
"Bill Gates has been unseated as the world's second-richest person. Here's how he spends his $129 billion fortune, from a luxury-car collection to incredible real estate."
www.businessinsider.com
https://www.businessinsider.com/billionaire-bill-gates-net-worth-spending-2018-8
(accessed February 3, 2021)

7. *Fl*avius Josephus, The Antiquities of the Jews
Book 1, Chapter 4, Paragraph 3
(accessed February 4, 2021)

8. Public Broadcasting Service
"Bonhoeffer"
www.pbs.org
https://www.pbs.org/bonhoeffer/timeline.html
(accessed February 4, 2021)

9. A&E Television Networks, History
"Anti-Nazi theologian Dietrich Bonhoeffer is hanged"
www.history.com
https://www.history.com/this-day-in-history/defiant-theologian-dietrich-bonhoeffer-is-hanged
(accessed February 6, 2021)

10. National Library of Medicine
"Role of abortion in control of global population growth"
National Center for Biotechnology Information
www.pubmed.gov
https://pubmed.ncbi.nlm.nih.gov/3709011/
(accessed February 6, 2021)

Chapter 2: Plans for a Global Reset

1. The Hill
"Introducing the 'Great Reset,' world leaders' radical plan to transform the economy"
www.thehill.com
https://thehill.com/opinion/energy-environment/504499-introducing-the-great-reset-world-leaders-radical-plan-to
(accessed February 10, 2021)

Chapter 3: Christians Facing the Courts of Babylon

1. Chabad—Virtual Jewish Library
"Why Is 70 Special?"
www.chabad.org
https://www.chabad.org/library/article_cdo/aid/940857/jewish/Why-is-70-special.htm
(accessed February 13, 2021)

Chapter 4: The Coming Persecution Against Christianity in America

1. Lexico, Powered by Oxford
   www.lexico.com
   https://www.lexico.com/definition/persecution
   (accessed February 14, 2021)

2. Geological Society of London Publications
   "The Bible and geology: destruction of Sodom and Gomorrah"
   Lyell Collection
   https://sp.lyellcollection.org/content/273/1/133
   (accessed February 16, 2021)

3. Wikipedia, The Free Encyclopedia
   "Plantation economy"
   www.wikipedia.org
   https://en.wikipedia.org/wiki/Plantation_economy
   (accessed February 22, 2021)

4. The Meredith Corporation
   "More People Moved to Tennessee in 2020 Than Any Other State, According to a New Report"
   www.people.com
   https://people.com/home/tennessee-welcomed-more-residents-any-state-2020-u-haul/
   (accessed February 22, 2021)

5. U.S. News
   "Most Religious States in America"
   www.usnews.com
   https://www.usnews.com/news/best-states/slideshows/10-most-religious-states-in-america?slide=9
   (accessed February 22, 2021)

6. Lifeway Christian Resources
"One State Dominates The Most Bible-Minded Cities List"
Resource Library
www.lifewayresource.com
https://lifewayresearch.com/2017/07/06/one-state-dominates-bible-minded-city-list/

Chapter 5: Should Christians Resist or Submit to a Corrupt Government?

1. Public Broadcasting Service
"The Church And The Revolutionary War"
www.pbs.org
https://www.pbs.org/opb/historydetectives/feature/the-church-and-the-revolutionary-war/
(accessed February 23, 2021)

2. The Library of Congress
"Religion and the Founding of the American Republic"
www.loc.gov
https://www.loc.gov/exhibits/religion/rel03.html
(accessed February 23, 2021)

3. American Battlefield Trust
"American Revolution Facts"
www.battlefields.org
https://www.battlefields.org/learn/articles/american-revolution-faqs
(accessed February 25, 2021)

Chapter 6: The Balaam Plot and America's Self-Curse

1. Spirit & Truth Fellowship International
   "Galatians"
   www.stfonline.org
   https://www.stfonline.org/pdf/rev/galatians_commentary.pdf
   (accessed February 27, 2021)

2. Wikipedia, The Free Encyclopedia
   "Anathema"
   www.wikipedia.org
   https://en.wikipedia.org/wiki/Anathema
   (accessed February 27, 2021)

Chapter 7: Necessary Resistance: Elijah and Jezebel— The Coming Clash

1. Bible Hub
   Englishman's Concordance
   www.biblehub.com
   https://biblehub.com/greek/strongs_646.htm
   (accessed February 27, 2021)

2. Wikipedia, The Free Encyclopedia
   "Revolution"
   www.wikipedia.org
   https://en.wikipedia.org/wiki/Revolution
   (accessed February 27, 2021)

Chapter 9: The Woman Who Would Be President

1. Carsales
   "12 cars that are shaped like eggs just in time for Easter"
   www.carsales.com
   https://www.carsales.com.au/editorial/details/12-cars-that-are-shaped-like-eggs-just-in-time-for-easter-117596/
   (accessed February 28, 2021)

2. Minnesota Public Radio
   Marketplace Tech
   "The next wave of driverless cars won't have pedals or steering wheels. Is that allowed?"
   www.marketplace.org
   https://www.marketplace.org/shows/marketplace-tech/the-next-wave-of-driverless-cars-wont-have-pedals-or-steering-wheels-is-that-allowed/
   (accessed February 28, 2021)

3. Title Max, History of the Autonomous Car
   "History of the Autonomous Car"
   www.titlemax.com
   https://www.titlemax.com/resources/history-of-the-autonomous-car/
   (accessed February 28, 2021)

4. Pietro D'Aloisio, Prophecies From The End Times
   (Taken from the messages of the prophet, William Branham)
   http://www.branham.it/joomla/documenti/lingue/prophecies.html
   (accessed February 28, 2021)

5. Medium
A Living Network of Curious Minds
"Our ideology score placed Kamala Harris as the most liberal senator in 2019; what kinds of bills has she introduced?"
govtrackinsider.com
https://govtrackinsider.com/our-ideology-score-placed-kamala-harris-as-the-most-liberal-senator-in-2019-bbd25493ca72
(accessed February 28, 2021)

6. Pietro D'Aloisio, Prophecies From The End Times
(Taken from the messages of the prophet, William Branham)
http://www.branham.it/joomla/documenti/lingue/prophecies.html
(accessed February 28, 2021)

Chapter 10: The Rise of the Trump Stump

1. Ducksters, Technological Solutions, INC
"Ancient Mesopotamia: Biography of Nebuchadnezzar II
https://www.ducksters.com/history/mesopotamia/nebuchadnezzar_ii.php
(accessed March 4, 2021)

2. Wikipedia, The Free Encyclopedia
"The Trump Organization"
www.wikipedia.org
https://en.wikipedia.org/wiki/The_Trump_Organization
(accessed March 4, 2021)

3. Cumulus Media, WBAP News Talk
"Rasmussen: Trump's Approval Rating Rises After DC Protests"
www.wbap.com
https://www.wbap.com/news/rasmussen-trumps-approval-rating-rises-after-dc-protests/
(accessed March 6, 2021)

Chapter 12: Silicon Valley: The Land of Sand

1. Wikipedia, The Free Encyclopedia
"Silicon Valley"
www.wikipedia.org
https://en.wikipedia.org/wiki/Silicon_Valley
(accessed March 6, 2021)

2. Bonnier Corporation Company, Popular Science
"Making Silicon from Sand"
www.popsci.com
https://www.popsci.com/diy/article/2005-10/making-silicon-sand/
(accessed March 6, 2021)

3. HZO, Inc.
"Corrosion: What is Water Damage Really Doing to Your Electronics?"
www.hzo.com
https://www.hzo.com/blog/corrosion-water-damage-electronics/
(accessed March 6, 2021)

Chapter 15: Has America Entered Her Fullness of Time?

1. Wikipedia, The Free Encyclopedia
"Roman roads"
www.wikipedia.org
https://en.wikipedia.org/wiki/Roman_roads
(accessed March 7, 2021)

2. Carol Ashby, Life in the Roman Empire
"The Roman Navy"
www.carolashby.com
https://carolashby.com/the-roman-navy/
(accessed March 7, 2021)

3. The Library of Congress
"Religion and the Founding of the American Republic"
www.loc.gov
https://www.loc.gov/exhibits/religion/rel02.html
(accessed March 7, 2021)

4. Statista Research Department
"How often do you attend church or synagogue - at least once a week, almost every week, about once a month, seldom, or never?"
www.statista.com
https://www.statista.com/statistics/245491/church-attendance-of-americans/
(accessed March 7, 2021)